Explo Supernatural Wales

Terror and Mystery in the Welsh Wilds

By Alvin Nicholas

Alvin Nicholas has been researching and collecting stories about 'frightening' supernatural sites in the British countryside for many years. He currently works as a countryside ranger, based in his native South Wales, and has a particular interest in all things relating to mountains. He is a Mountain Leader Award holder, and has many years of experience of helping people to enjoy the countryside. If you have a story about a supernatural rural location anywhere in the British Isles, he would like to hear from you. Alvin can be contacted by email at adsn9@hotmail.com.

Acknowledgements

Special thanks go to Ingrid and to the many others who have helped with this project, both wittingly and unwittingly. Special thanks also to Anne and Michael for use of their home as the North Wales 'expedition base', and to Sarah for putting up with my fascination for all things supernatural.

Landmark Publishing

═══════Published by═══════

Ashbourne Hall, Cokayne Ave
Ashbourne, Derbyshire, DE6 1EJ England
Tel: (01335) 347349 Fax: (01335) 347303
e-mail: landmark@clara.net

1st Edition

13 ISBN: 978-1-84306-337-7

10 ISBN: 1-84306-337-9

British Library Cataloguing in Publication Data: a catalogue record for this book is available from the British Library.

Print: Cromwell Press
Design by: Sarah Labuhn

All photographs were supplied by the author

Exploring Supernatural Wales

Terror and Mystery in the Welsh Wilds

By Alvin Nicholas

Dedication

For Ellis, Harriet and my parents

Landmark Publishing

Contents

Distribution of Walks

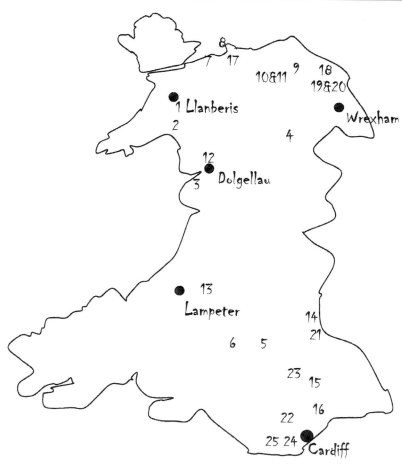

Route Map Key

⌃‾ Summit

Walk follows Public Right of Way / permitted route /
crosses Access Land   ▬ ▬ ▬ ▬

Other routes   ·············

Road   ▬▬▬▬▬

Walk follows road   ▬▬▬▬▬
  →

Introduction

I'll follow you, I'll lead you about a round, Through bog, through bush, through brake through brier, Sometime a horse I'll be, sometime a hound, A hog, a headless bear, sometime a fire; And neigh, and bark, and grunt, and roar, and burn, Like horse, hound, hog, bear, fire, at every turn (From *A Midsummer Night's Dream* – Act III Sc 1)

After many years reading about the mysteries and folklore of rural Wales, the motivation to finally write a book came in the African bush. At the time, I was working as a field ranger and living in a wooden hut in the middle of nowhere, feeling a little homesick.

One evening I began a debate with a native African colleague and good friend. Over drinks in 'the hut', after a nerve-wracking but exhilarating night spent patrolling the African bush, I lamented the fact that we in Wales had lost all of our most recent 'dangerous' big wildlife. Our 'Big Five' – brown bear, wolf, lynx, wild boar and aurochs (wild ox) – had become extinct hundreds, and in some cases thousands, of years ago.

That one did not have to fear an evening camping or walking in the Welsh 'wilds' was a source of some amusement to my colleague. How could a night in the Welsh countryside compare to the sheer exhilaration of Africa, when every nerve fibre is alert to the dangers that may lurk in the darkness – lion, leopard, elephant, buffalo, hyena, rhino and so on?

I thought about this carefully, and then made a bold statement: 'Given a choice, there are places in the Welsh countryside that would be more frightening to spend the night at than the wildest African bush.' My friend smiled and said, 'How could that be?'

You will not find many haunted buildings, charming folk tales or benign spectral beings within this book. It is a book about supernatural 'wild', lonely and frightening places in the countryside. If you are very brave, you may want to explore these places yourself; experiencing locations that evoke a primal fear of the unknown yet are irresistibly fascinating.

It is said that J R R Tolkien, author of *The Lord of the Rings*, yearned for the time of the old haunted countryside. Growing up in the Birmingham area, the countryside he saw around him was beautiful but tamed, and, unlike the countryside of the distant past, it was very safe. He imagined an ancient and dangerous landscape of haunted mountains, woods and other wild places. To all intents and purposes, he imagined Wales.

Moonlit camps on rolling moor, sinister woods where dark forces conspire, mountains and valleys where strange 'things' reside for evermore. This book is dedicated to the supernatural 'wild' places of Wales: the haunted mountains, moors, hills and woods.

'Spookscapes'

Nature and human culture have conspired within Wales to create one of the most fascinating and diverse landscapes in the world. Human interaction with the land resulted in the many elements of the countryside we see today. Our woods, fields and hedgerows were 'carved' out of the primeval landscape. The 'current' countryside is evidence of our ancestors' close association with the land.

Obvious traces of the long human occupation of Wales abound. To the keen eye, the hand of man can be found almost everywhere: ancient field patterns, Bronze Age barrows, standing stones and Iron Age hill forts to name but a fraction. Look out into the darkness of a seemingly empty landscape and one must realise that people (and animals) have lived, worshiped and died in these places for many thousands of years.

Past peoples developed a close association with the landscape. It was a place full of meaning and some places inevitably gained a reputation as 'sacred' or 'special' in some way. Before the advent of modern archaeology many archaeological remains were interpreted as supernatural in nature and origin. This was particularly true of remains whose origin lay in the dim and very distant past. 'Fairy mounds' (often Bronze Age barrows) are a prominent example of this phenomenon.

As will become evident, historical associations seem to be an important factor at some of the more notorious supernatural sites. Many seem to be near to archaeological features, and most seem to have a long history of myth and legend or are associated with tragic events.

Is the key ingredient human interaction? If there is indeed something to this then it can't be past human interaction alone or almost everywhere would be haunted.

What is special about our haunted places? In the context of this book we must also consider that some sites may have 'always' been the location of inexplicable events, and were later associated with contemporary folklore – fairy folk for one generation, extraterrestrials for the next.

Are they 'gateways' to knowledge that has so far eluded rational science? Read on, explore and maybe you will discover some answers.

The Walks

After each of the main featured stories, you will find a suggested walk along with a basic map and other useful information. The emphasis is very much on *access* to supernatural places and landscapes.

I have resisted the temptation to include unnecessary circular routes unless they genuinely make the walk more convenient and/or interesting. This approach means that you will find an unusually diverse range of walk types in the book. You can choose from short linear walks, part-circular routes and full circular walks, depending on the nature of the location.

All walks are graded according to the level of fitness required and the complexity of terrain. The grades are:

Easy: Gentle/undulating terrain, suitable for occasional walkers.

Moderate: Walks that include longer ascents/descents. These walks are suitable for regular walkers.

Energetic: Some steep ascents/descents over longer distances in remote terrain. Suitable for more experienced hill-walkers with good navigation skills.

You should never rely solely on the sketch maps provided in this book. Always take a good quality (preferably a detailed 1:25,000 / 1:50,000) map and a compass, especially when walking in remote or mountainous terrain.

Remember that walks in the countryside always require a degree of common sense and judgement and are never completely free of risk. Be prepared and take adequate provisions, equipment and clothing.

Always be aware of the consequences of a slip or fall on steep or mountainous terrain. Be prepared for changes in weather conditions and know the weather forecast. Some sections cross busy roads so take care, and remember that traffic can be a danger even on quiet country lanes.

About the Book

The structure of the book

At the beginning of the book, you will find an 'A–Z' of the supernatural countryside, which I have called 'Supernatural History'. This is an eclectic mix of terms and concepts of relevance to the book, designed to enhance your knowledge of mysteries both old and new.

Each of the reviewed sites has been assigned to one of three broad 'types' of countryside. These are 'The High Mountains', 'Lonely Moors and Sinister Hills' and 'Haunted Woods and Wooded Lanes'. You will also find a section on 'Further Exploration' in each category, in which you will find information about sites that could be interesting, but are not included as walks in the book.

In each section the stories start in the north and end in the south, and represent what I feel are the most supernatural sites and landscapes in rural Wales.

If you want to experience something mysterious, inexplicable or downright frightening, the information contained within should help you on your way. As the minimalist explorer and naturalist John Muir once said, 'throw a loaf of bread and a pound of tea in an old sack and jump over the back fence'. So get your walking boots on. 'They' are waiting for you. I hope you enjoy the journey!

Supernatural History

The following A–Z will aid your exploration of supernatural Wales.

AFANC: A large and deadly mountain lake monster from Welsh mythology. The afanc is sometimes thought be demonic in nature. Anyone entering a lake inhabited by an afanc is likely to be devoured. A terrifying afanc once inhabited Glaslyn, a lake below the east face of Snowdon. The afanc was seen as recently as the 1930s when some climbers observed it raise its head above the surface of the lake before submerging.

ALIEN BIG CAT (ABC): Alien Big Cats are said to be non-native, large predatory cats. The most commonly sighted is the 'black panther', which is thought to be a melanistic (black) leopard. It is thought that the licensing system brought in by the Dangerous Wild Animals Act (1976) led to owners of large cats releasing their 'beloved pets' into the wild. An apparent rise in sightings seems to indicate that these animals are breeding.

Some speculate that Alien Big Cats are less than flesh and blood and somehow related to age-old sightings of **BLACK DOGS AND WEREWOLVES**, particularly in the light of their usual black colour and fondness for similar 'habitats' – country lanes, lonely moors etc.

ANNWN: The Celtic Underworld/Otherworld, to which doorways can be found in the physical world. Gateways to the Underworld are most often found in hills, mountains and mountain lakes.

ARAWN: In Welsh Celtic mythology, Arawn is the King of ANNWN, the Celtic Underworld (see above).

BALL LIGHTNING: Ball lightning is a rare phenomenon, thought to be associated with thunderstorms. Glowing, floating spherical objects have been reported, varying in size from that of a golf ball to the more common basketball size.

Although similar effects have been recreated in laboratories, the bizarre characteristics of ball lightning mean that the phenomenon is still a mystery. There are thousands of reports of ball lightning entering buildings (sometimes leaving spherical holes in glass windows), 'chasing' people, and generally causing mayhem.

One theory states that ball lightning is

9

highly ionised plasma held together by its own magnetic fields, another is that the balls consist of silicon vapour from soil while, more recently, it has also been suggested that 'primordial mini black holes' are the core energy source. The last theory developed as a result of the characteristics of one particularly well-documented ball-lightning event in Donegal, Ireland in 1868. The 2ft ball exhibited inexplicable energy for its size. It lasted for 20 minutes and had enough energy to create a 100m trench through a peat bog.

Ball lightning has been associated with supernatural phenomena such as UFO's, poltergeists, GHOSTS and the appearance of BLACK DOGS.

BARROW: Sometimes used interchangeably with CAIRN, but usually refers to a prehistoric burial chamber or deposit that is covered with earth. In folklore, barrows are sometimes associated with supernatural occurrences/entities such as BLACK DOGS.

BIGFOOT: See MAN-BEAST.

BLACK DOG: See GWYLLGI.

BRENIN LLWYD: The Brenin Llwyd, 'Grey King' or 'Monarch of the Mist' is said to sit amongst the high mountains clothed in a grey cloud of mist. He would lie in wait to ensnare those lost amongst the mountain peaks, and until fairly recently the mountain guides of Snowdonia were said to be wary of an encounter with this entity.

The Brenin Llwyd has parallels with reports of MAN-BEASTS and may be related to the Am Fear Liath Mòr or 'Big Grey Man' of Ben MacDui, Scotland.

BROCKEN SPECTRE: The 'Spectre of Brocken' is named after sightings on the Brocken, the highest peak in Germany's Harz Mountains. It appears when a low sun is behind a climber looking down into mist from a peak or ridge. The effect can be spectacular, and sometimes the shadow of the climber cast into the mist can be huge and frightening. A glowing halo effect associated with the phenomenon is known as a 'glory'.

BWBACH: A goblin, ghost or spectre, sometimes associated with places, e.g. Lôn y Bwbach (Goblin/Ghost Lane). Bwbach can be found almost anywhere in the Welsh countryside.

BWCI: A goblin, ghost or spectre, sometimes associated with places, e.g. Carreg y Bwci (Goblin/Ghost Stone).

BWGAN: A goblin, ghost or spectre, sometimes associated with places, e.g. Carreg y Bwgan) (Goblin/Ghost Stone). Classified by Wirt Sikes as a good-natured Goblin, though they may have a dual character.

CAIRN: A BARROW consisting of a round/long mound of stones. Cairns are most often found in the upland areas of western and northern Britain. They sometimes contain a burial in a cist, which is a square/rectangular burial chamber. Bronze Age cairns can be confused with Clearance Cairns, which were created through agricultural clearance, as well as cairns constructed by hill-walkers and others.

CAIRN CIRCLE: A ring of stones surrounding a CAIRN. Often the cairn is destroyed, leaving a ring of stones that looks like a STONE CIRCLE.

CANWYLL CORFF: The Welsh word for CORPSE CANDLE.

CARRIAGE (SPECTRAL): The ghostly sound of a carriage is a common reported phenomenon on many country roads. Often (but not necessarily) associated with the site of a tragedy.

CELT: First recorded by the Greeks as the 'Keltoi', the Celts were central Europeans with a similar language, religion and culture. The Celts were not centrally governed, and gradually infiltrated Britain between about 500 and 100 BC. The Celtic peoples are distinct from earlier (pre-Iron Age) native Britons. The word 'Celt' is often confused with 'Druid' (See DRUID).

COBLYNAU: The Coblynau are spectral dwarfs whose preferred habitat is the mines of mountainous regions.

CORPSE CANDLE: This is a spectral light, which in Wales is often associated with death. In Tolkien's *Lord of the Rings,* the hobbits are led by Gollum through 'The Dead Marshes' – the site of a great battle and haunted by 'The Tricksey Lights' which are the 'candles of corpses'. See also SPOOKLIGHT and SPIRIT PATH.

CROMLECH: A burial chamber with three or more upright stones and one or more capstones. Also known as a Dolmen.

CROP CIRCLE: These are areas of crop that have been flattened to produce geometric shapes. The phenomenon has been observed for hundreds of years, but the increasing complexity of crop circles has led to suspicion that most are of human origin. The debate continues.

CWN ANNWN: ARAWN is said to ride with his white, red-eared spectral Hounds of Hell (the Cŵn Annwn or Hounds of Annwn) through the skies at certain times of the year, particularly autumn and winter. Strangely, their growling is louder when they are at a distance, and as they draw near the growling grows quieter. The legend of the Wild Hunt, as it is known in England, is widspread throughout Britain and Europe. In England, the hunter is said to be Herne, named after the antlered ghost of Windsor Forest, whilst in parts of Europe he is Odin, Norse father of the gods. The hunt is most often seen on dark, stormy nights.

CYHIRAETH: The Welsh name for a banshee. Her wail is a portent of death or disaster. May be related to the GWRACH Y RHYBIN.

DEVIL: The Devil was once very active in the Welsh countryside, as evidenced by numerous landforms, bridges etc. attributed to his activities.

DRAGON: Dragons may be associated with symbolism, power, landforms and earth energies, as well as physical (usually reptilian) creatures. Physical land dragons are recorded in folklore all over Wales (the most famous being the perpetually fighting dragons of Dinas Emrys in North Wales). The 'gwiber' (Welsh for viper) was the most common type of dragon in Wales. It was a highly venomous creature, and looked like a legless winged snake. Water dragons (afancs) were also very numerous (see AFANC). Some think dragon legends could be associated with EARTH LIGHTS.

DRUID: The Druids were Iron Age (Celtic) priests and guardians/implementers of unwritten customary law. Emperor Claudius 'banned' the Druids in AD 60. The Romans decided that the only way to eliminate the Druids was to attack their heartland – the island of Anglesey – in the hope that if the centre of their power was destroyed, those in outlying areas would die out.

The power and influence of the Druids has led to many supernatural phenomena being attributed to them, long after their disapearence. Some thought that FAIRIES were the spirits of long-dead Druids, denied access to the Christian heaven.

EARTH LIGHT: Strange lights seen in the landscape or the skies are sometimes categorised as 'earth lights'. It is thought that these lights are associated with earthquakes, as reports of strange lights and earthquakes often coincide. There is evidence for increased earth light and UFO activity along known geological faults. More detailed information can be found in two books by earth light researcher Paul Devereux, called *Earth Lights* and *Earth Lights Revelation*.

A problem with this theory is that some locations seem to produce earth lights 'to time', especially on one of the 'spirit nights' of May Day eve, Midsummer Eve and Midwinter Eve (Cadair Idris is a good example – see *The High Mountains*).

ELLYLL (pl. ELLYLLON): In *British Goblins*, Wirt Sikes describes the Ellyllon thus: 'The Ellyllon are the pigmy elves who haunt the groves and valleys, and correspond pretty closely with the English elves. The English name was probably derived from the Welsh el, a spirit, elf, an element.' Ellyll can sometimes refer to a ghost, goblin or demon.

ELLYLLDAN: The Ellylldan are said to correspond to the English Will-o'-the-wisp of marshy ground. The word translates as 'elf fire'. See also SPOOK LIGHT.

FAIRY: See TYLWYTH TEG.

FAIRY RING: A circular pattern, usually seen in grass, once thought to be caused by dancing fairies. At least some were caused by fungi, but others were more mysterious and could be related to CROP CIRCLES. Rural folk were terrified of fairy rings because of the danger of being abducted and transported to the fairy realm.

GHOST: Assuming they are real, then to understand the nature of ghosts may help us understand our own true nature and place in the universe. Some feel a complete theory could even enhance our understanding of the universe itself. The problem is that our understanding of ghosts is minimal, and for most they will remain frightening, mysterious or a figment of an overactive imagination.

Various attempts have been made to categorise ghosts. In the context of this book, we are mainly interested in ghosts that seem to be associated with certain places, in our case mountains, moors, hills and woods. One of the problems is the sheer range of ghost 'types.' The spirits of the dead, phantom aeroplanes, spectral coaches and BLACK DOGS have all been referred to as 'ghosts'. What follows is a brief overview of some of the many theories relating to the nature and origin of ghosts.

The 'stone tape' theory is amongst the most well-known attempts at explaining ghosts. The theory holds that at certain conditions, actual events are 'recorded' in the surrounding environment, rather like a tape recording. When conditions allow, the events are played back to the observer who witnesses the event or part of the event as it occurred.

The 'playback' mechanism remains a mystery, but certain ghostly accounts seem to generally fit the theory. Phantom armies are one of the most obvious examples. In Wales, some of the most common accounts refer to Roman soldiers and the sounds of marching feet.

One of the most intriguing 'forgotten' theories relating to ghostly encounters was put forward by Tom Lethbridge. Lethbridge trained as an archaeologist and historian, and most of his working life was spent as a Keeper of Anglo-Saxon Antiquities at the University Museum in Cambridge. In his later years he moved to an old Tudor house in Devon.

After a number of strange experiences relating to a 'witch' living next door and unusual experiences in wet/damp locations, he began to wonder if water was the key to understanding ghosts. He wondered if the static electric field of water could somehow 'record' strong emotions. When a sensitive person steps into the field, the 'recorded' events could be sensed or heard. This could explain why some ghosts seem to appear in damp or stormy conditions, near rivers, lakes and wells.

In *Ghosts and Legends of Wales* J A Brookes tells the story of a Black Dog sighting in a forest near Tufton at the foot of the Preseli Mountains. A twelve-year-old boy and an Englishman by the name of Ron Stevens were training hawks near an old cottage. Suddenly, a large black dog emerged from the undergrowth. Mr Stevens told the boy to 'shoo' it away, which he attempted to do. At that instant a big black woman rose up in front of his eyes with a black hat on her head. Her top teeth curled over her bottom lip, and although her clothes were all black her teeth were white. 'Her hands were encased, as though in gloves, and were tight across her chest.' The woman wore large black boots with curled-up toes. She appeared to smile at the pair and seemed to beckon them to follow. This they did, and after following her for a short while the frightened witnesses claimed she disappeared into an old well. When they looked into the well, the water was still and undisturbed.

Of course, the various 'stone tape' theories are unsatisfactory when it comes to the many cases of ghosts that purposefully interact with the living, and a further problem arises when one tries to account for the 'ghosts' of inanimate objects such as aeroplanes and carriages.

One theory holds that ghosts are somehow related to the nature of time, which isn't as 'linear' as one would think. There are numerous reports of time slips, where individuals not only witness past events, but are also briefly transported to a different place and time. I can recall a story I once read about a man who claimed to see the ghost of an old man in his home. Through the use of a technique known as automatic writing, the man established contact with the 'ghost', which proceeded to beg the man to stop communicating with him as 'people were beginning to talk'. As far as the 'ghost' was concerned, it was the present and he was alive. The man from the future was as much a 'ghost' to him as he was to the man. In *Time Storms*, Jenny Randles puts forward the theory that 'holes in time' occur on a regular basis and result in a whole host of strange phenomena.

I myself experienced something strange one

evening. At the time, I was living in a very old house, and decided to undertake an experiment with a tape recorder. I was inspired to undertake the experiment after reading about 'electronic voice phenomena', popularised by the film *White Noise*. To cut a long story short, there are innumerable cases of people making tape recordings in allegedly haunted (and non-haunted) locations, playing the tape and finding strange voices on the tape. Sometimes the voices seem to convey an intelligent message. I went down to a basement room (which I rarely used), switched on the tape recorder and asked, 'Is anyone there?' I waited for a minute and asked, 'What is your name?' I went back upstairs to the living room and played back the tape. Now it is worth stating that I checked the tape was completely blank before I made the recording. I wasn't really expecting anything to be on the tape, but when I played it back, after I asked if anyone was there, a chillingly clear response issued from the recorder. Immediately after my question, the word 'Hello?' came across clearly and distinctly. The voice was totally different to my own. It sounded like it was being said in reverse, rather like a tape being played backwards, yet the word was clear. As you can imagine, this sent a shiver of excitement and fear through my body. The recording continued. After I asked, 'What is your name?' the response came immediately. It sounded like 'Baron' or something similar. The voice and tone were the same as before.

The reason I have included this little story is that it may have implications for your exploration of the supernatural countryside. With a reasonably cheap dictaphone you can undertake your own 'investigations' of the sites within this book. After my experience, I can say with some confidence that this method works. Whether electronic voice phenomena represent communication across time, communication with the dead or even communication with your own subconscious mind is a total mystery.

Poltergeists are often categorised separately from ghosts, even though the separation is speculative. The word 'poltergeist' is derived from two German words: *polter,* meaning noisy, and *geist,* meaning ghost or spirit. They are known for making noises, throwing objects and generally causing havoc. Poltergeists have

been recorded for hundreds of years. In general, 'outbreaks' seem to centre on unhappy or stressed individuals, particularly teenagers. One would imagine this means poltergeists are somehow linked to a hitherto unknown mechanism whereby the human mind can move objects, cause sounds and so forth, through what is known as psychokinesis.

However, as is usual with the paranormal, the phenomenon seems to be far more complicated. Sometimes, the poltergeist seems to have independent existence separate from the suspected 'troubled mind,' and, as with the famous case of the 'Enfield poltergeist', may claim to be the spirit of a deceased person who then gives information which can be checked through records, relatives etc.

In the astounding case of the 'Cardiff poltergeist' there were no adolescent children and no emotional problems. 'Pete', as the poltergeist was known, haunted a lawnmower repair shop and seemed to display independent intelligence, playfulness and responsiveness, and had a penchant for throwing stones.

The complications continue. A further theory attempts to account for spectral animals, man-beasts, werewolves, ghosts and many other supernatural entities. The theory was recently brought back to the fore in Nick Redfern's highly entertaining book, *Three Men Seeking Monsters: Six Weeks in Pursuit of Werewolves, Lake Monsters, Giant Cats, Ghostly Devil Dogs, and Ape-Men*. The theory refers to 'tulpas', a Tibetan term which refers to an entity that attains a form of reality after being created through imagination alone (the theory will be of particular inertest those who have read *Sophie's World* by Jostein Gaarder). The creation of a tulpa is supposed to be possible through mental training, but the tulpa can attain independent physical reality and act of its own volition, sometimes against the creator's will.

In the book, a certain 'Mother Sarah' informs the author that a group known as 'the Nine' invoked specific tulpas, which she called 'Cormons'. The intention was for the entities to defend ancient Britain from 'marauding invaders'. The Cormons were invoked anman- ancient stone circle on Dartmoor, but killed their creators. Soon after, sightings of MAN-BEASTS, spectral dogs and other weird entities were reported the length and breadth of the country. The Cormons were free to roam independently, beyond mortal control.

Although the story may sound a bit tongue in cheek, it is worth considering the following case. In 1972 an experiment was undertaken by the Toronto Society for Psychical Research. The aim of the group was to see if they could 'create' a ghost. The group wrote a completely fictitious 'history' of a ghost. The setting for the story was Diddington Manor, Warwickshire. Although the house was real, the name was altered for the experiment.

The group invented a seventeenth-century aristocrat called Philip, as well as a detailed story regarding his tragic life. The group undertook meticulous research in order to furnish Philip with a believable history. After a few weeks a variety of poltergeist- like phenomena began, and the group were able to communicate with Philip, who was able to provide the group with details of his made-up existence through rapping sounds. The group had 'created' a ghost.

As will have become evident, we don't *really* understand ghosts. All we know is that there are likely to be many 'answers', none of them straightforward. Perhaps we should take more at face value. Ghosts are the spirits of the dead, and they're out there, waiting!

GOBLIN: Goblins are usually described as evil or mischevous beings of variable height that look like 'grotesque gnomes'.

GWRACH: The Welsh word for 'witch' or 'hag.'

GWRACH Y RHYBIN: A form of Welsh banshee. Her name means 'Hag of the Warning'. Like the CYHIRAETH, she sometimes warns of a death and is often encountered at a crossroads or stream. Sometimes she is referred to as the 'Hag of the Mountains' or 'Hag of the Mist'.

In South Wales, she appears as a poor old woman with an oblong, four-cornered hat. In *A Relation of Apparitions of Spirits in the County of Monmouth and the Principality of Wales*, Reverend Edmund Jones ('Old Prophet' Jones, as he was known) gives a lucid description: 'The Apparition was the resemblance of a poor old woman, with an oblong four-cornered hat, ash-coloured clothes, her apron thrown a-cross her shoulder, with a pot or wooden can in her hand, such as poor people carry to fetch milk with, always going before them, sometimes crying out wow up. Who ever saw this Apparition, whether by night or in a misty day, though well acquainted with the road, they would be sure to lose their way; for the road appeared quite different to what it really was; and so far sometimes the fascination was, that they thought they were going to their journey's end when they were really going the contrary way. Sometimes they heard her cry wow up, when they did not see her.'

In *Folk-Lore and Folk-Stories of Wales*, Marie Trevelyan says, 'This spectral form is described as having long black hair, black eyes, and a swarthy countenance. Sometimes one of her eyes is grey and the other black. Both are deeply sunken and piercing. Her back was crooked, her figure was very thin and spare, and her pigeon-breasted bust was concealed by a sombre scarf. Her trailing robes were black. She was sometimes seen with long flapping wings that fell heavily at her sides, and occasionally she went flying low down along watercourses, or around hoary mansions. Frequently the flapping of her leathern bat-like wings could be heard against the window-panes.'

The Gwrach y Rhybin has parallels in other parts of Britain. In Leicestershire she is 'Black Annis' or 'Anna' – a savage hag with great teeth and long nails who devoured human victims. In Derbyshire she is known as 'T'owd woman', whilst in the Scottish Highlands she is the 'Cailleach'. The hag has many parallels with HECATE. There is at least one case of a BLACK DOG transforming into a hag (which then disappeared down a well – see GHOST for more information on this case).

GWRAGEDD ANNWN: The Gwragedd Annwn are the Wives of the Underworld or Hell and dwell in wild and lonely mountain lakes, the most famous being Llyn y Fan Fach in the Camarthen Fans (Brecon Beacons National Park).

GWYLLGI: Gwyllgi are also known as Dogs of Darkness, Hell Hounds or Hounds of Destiny, but most commonly as Black Dogs. Black Dogs have been seen for centuries, and can be distinguished from flesh and blood dogs by numerous supernatural characteristics. These include glowing eyes (most often red), the ability to appear and vanish into thin air and the ability to change their size and appearance.

They are found throughout Britain, and regional names include 'Black Shuck', 'Guytrash,, 'Shriker' and 'Barguest.' They tend to haunt country roads (particularly crossroads), old trackways and stiles and are the guardians of ancient burial mounds and other prehistoric sites. Examples include West Kennet burial mound in Wiltshire, Doghill Barrow near Stonehenge, and an 'artificial circle' between Amlwch and St Elian's Church, Anglesey.

A sinister Gwyllgi haunts a field called Cot-Mor in Pembrokeshire, 'where two stones are set up, called the Devil's Nags.' Another haunts a place called Pant y Madog – 'a pit by the side of the lane leading to Laugharn, filled with water and not quite dry in summer.' According to Edmund Jones, this particular Gwyllgi terrified a woman with its unearthly 'earth moving' scream.

Water features in many Gwyllgi and Black Dog sightings. The phenomenon favours bridges, rivers and the coast (for more information on water and the supernatural see GHOST). This may have some bearing on why Black Dogs are sometimes associated with electrical storms and BALL LIGHTNING. Many feel Black Dogs are associated with boundaries, LEY LINES and SPIRIT PATHS.

GWYN AP NUDD: A king of the Underworld or ANNWN, also referred to as the king of the fairies.

HAG OF THE MOUNTAINS/MIST: See GWRACH Y RHYBIN.

HECATE: Originally a goddess of the wilderness and childbirth, Hecate or Hekate later became the 'queen of ghosts', and is often seen as a goddess of magic, the night, witchcraft and Wicca. Highways, crossroads and wild places are associated with Hecate. Her companions include apparitions and spectral dogs.

HELL HOUND: See CWN ANNWN and GWYLLGI.

HILL FORT: Iron Age hill forts can be

thought of as Wales's first functioning 'towns'. They were basically hilltop settlements, fortified by the use of ramparts and ditches.

HORSE (SPECTRAL): The disembodied sound of galloping horses is a fairly common ghostly phenomenon in the countryside. There are a number of reports of spectral riders, with and without heads!

JACK-O'-LANTERN: See SPOOKLIGHTS and CORPSE CANDLE.

LEY LINE: The subject of much speculation, ley lines are seen by some as straight hypothetical lines connecting geographical and historic points. The term 'ley' came from Alfred Watkins, a Herefordshire Brewer who noticed that ancient man-made features such as churches, stone circles, cairns, tumuli and prehistoric camps often seemed to be in alignment on maps.

His book, *The Old Straight Track*, made his theories public. Watkins speculated that in ancient times, when Britain had been far more densely forested, navigation was made easier by straight-line routes connecting prominent geographical points. These alignments include megalithic sites and ancient trading routes. More recent New Age theories suggest ley lines are the channels for a mysterious power. Dowsers are said to be able to sense the generally benign 'energy' found along ley lines. However, it is said that sometimes they are out of balance and can carry negative energies and are then termed 'black streams'.

Recent theories suggest that GHOSTS, BLACK DOGS etc. travel along ley lines, and some feel there is a connection between UFOs and leys, in particular where the lines converge.

MAN-BEAST: Man-beasts are human-shaped hairy creatures resembling Bigfoot, often exhibiting supernatural attributes such as glowing red eyes and extraordinary speed. Witnesses often report feeling an indescribable terror when in proximity to these creatures.

Since a number of man-beasts have been seen in Britain, which is far to small to host an undiscovered primate, it is thought these creatures must be less than flesh and blood. See also BRENIN LLYWYD.

ORB: Orbs are thought to be the early stages of a ghost manifestation. It is thought that ghosts take the form of a small ball of light (sometimes transparent) because it is the most energy-efficient. Orbs are easily photographed using a digital camera, though the subject is controversial. Particles of dust can easily be mistaken for orbs.

PAGANISM: A non-Christian religion or nature worship.

PREHISTORIC WALES: Human history in Wales begins around 225,000 years ago in the Lower Palaeolithic period (Old Stone Age).

Mesolithic: The Middle Stone Age, between the Palaeolithic and the Neolithic from 8300 BC to 4000 BC. During this period, Mesolithic hunter-gatherers inhabited Wales.

Neolithic: The New Stone Age, from around 4000 BC to 2200 BC, was the period that saw major clearance of the wildwood and the earliest farming communities in Wales.

Bronze Age: From around 2200 BC to 800 BC, a period characterised by the use of bronze for the manufacture of weapons and tools. The climate was warmer in Wales than the present day, allowing the utilisation of the uplands.

Iron Age: This is the final prehistoric period. The period lasted from around 800 BC to the Roman occupation in AD 43. The use of iron superseded the use of bronze for the production of tools, utensils and weaponry. This period is characterised by the building of hill forts – Wales's earliest 'towns'.

PUCK: Puck is the English word for PWCA/PWCCA and is a shape-shifting Will-o'-the-wisp, fairy, hobgoblin or imp. He is also known as Robin Goodfellow. Puck was immortalised in William Shakespeare's *A Midsummer Night's Dream* (see 'A Midsummer Night's Nightmare' in *Haunted Woods and Wooded Lanes*). **PWCA,**

PWCA, PWCCA: Pwca, Pwcca or Pooka is another name for the ELLYLLDAN, as Puck is another name for the Will-o'-the-wisp. The term was used generically to refer to a goblin or fairy.

SACRED GROVE: The DRUIDS did not meet in temples or other stone structures. Instead, they met in sacred groves of trees, otherwise known as nemeton.

SPOOK LIGHT: Spook lights are found throughout the world. The most famous are the Brown Mountain lights of North Carolina, the Marfa spook lights in Texas and the Joplin spook lights of Missouri.

The English Jack-o'-Lantern or Will-o'-the-wisp is a spectral light most often associated with marshy or boggy ground, particularly in the uplands. They were a relatively common sight in the dark Welsh countryside of old, but are probably the victims of modern-day light pollution and habitat destruction. In former days, these lights were felt to be mischievous spirits intent on leading the night-time traveller astray.

It has been postulated that such lights are the result of the combustion of methane released from boggy ground, but many defy such simple categorisation, and some seem to display some sort of intelligent intent. The best places to see a Will o' the wisp are the bogs of the Black Mountains in South Wales and the marshes of the Point of Ayr, near Talacre in Flintshire.

I myself witnessed what may have been a Will-o'-the-wisp one dark night in a marshy hollow, in the middle of a large field. There could be no doubt that the field was completely deserted. Every time I tried to approach the light, it disappeared.

Illustrating the difficulties of classification, some of the most famous spook lights were known as the 'Egryn Lights'. These appeared in Wales during the 1905 Welsh religious revival and seemed to be centred on a prominent local preacher by the name of Mary Jones. The lights took the form of low-altitude aerial lights, verified by numerous independent witnesses. The lights had a particular habit of appearing over chapels when Jones was due to preach.

Spook lights may be related to BALL LIGHTNING, EARTH LIGHTS and UFOs.

SPIRIT PATH: Linear routes including prehistoric alignments and straight paths to and from cemeteries may be linked to an ancient belief that spirits travel in straight lines. Coffins used to be taken along these paths to be buried, sometimes in the belief that if this wasn't done correctly, bad things would happen. Spirit paths may be associated with LEY LINES.

STANDING STONE: A vertically placed

stone. Most are prehistoric in origin.

STONE CIRCLE: A ring of standing stones (not necessarily circular).

STONE ROW: A line of regularly spaced standing stones.

TREES (HAUNTED): Certain trees were considered sacred and/or magical in antiquity. They include oak, ash, hawthorn, holly, elder, rowan and yew. Oaks were of particular importance to the DRUIDS, and are often associated with FAIRIES. The yew can often be found in graveyards and is associated with the dead. It seems that, just like an old building, a tree can be haunted. Famous haunted trees include Ceubren yr Ellyl or the 'Hollow Tree of the Demon/Goblin' – an old oak which once stood in the Nannau Estate (see *Lonely Moors and Sinister Hills*). In *Mysterious Wales*, Chris Barber devotes a section to 'Terrible Trees'. Included are the 'bleeding yew' of Nevern and the 'Newcastle Oak' of Newcastle, South Wales, which was once possessed by an evil spirit.

TYLWYTH TEG: The Welsh word for fairies, meaning 'fair folk'. In South Wales, fairies were sometimes known as the Bendith y Mamau, meaning 'the mothers' blessing.' Some think the Tylwyth Teg are nature spirits, others that they are the souls of dead DRUIDS not bad enough for hell nor good enough for heaven. The Tylwyth Teg are said to be doomed to live on earth, and to dwell in its secret places until resurrection day.

An alternative theory holds that the Tylwyth Teg represent a 'race memory' of the mysterious ways and material remains of earlier Mesolithic/Neolithic or Bronze Age peoples of Britain. It has also been suggested that fairy sightings are the ghostly ceremonial re-enactments of the activities of earlier cultures, and this is why so many sightings revolve around STANDING STONES, BARROWS and other funerary and ritual monuments typical of so-called 'ritual landscapes'. Some feel that yesterday's 'fairies' are today's 'aliens' – an updated version of an ancient phenomenon.

TYLWYTH TEG YN Y COED: The 'fair folk in the wood', i.e. woodland fairies.

TYLWYTH TEG Y MWYN : The 'fair folk of the mine', i.e. mine fairies. The Tylwyth Teg y Mwyn were common in the ancient mines of Llanymynech Hill, near Welshpool.

UNIDENTIFIED FLYING OBJECT (UFO): A UFO is an object or light whose appearance, trajectory and behaviour doesn't suggest a logical, conventional explanation. A UFO is not automatically extraterrestrial in origin – it is merely an unidentified aerial 'thing.'

In *UFOs and How to See Them*, Jenny Randles identifies six of the most common UFO types:

1) The amber gambler. An orange, yellow or red ball of light. Seen regularly in 'window areas' (see WINDOW AREA).

2) The flying football. This is an egg- or oval-shaped object, which may be a variety of colours. This type of UFO is seen day and night and is associated with vehicle interference, physical effects and humming/generator-type sounds presumed to be energy emissions.

3) The cigar tube. This type of UFO is seen almost everywhere, and is often a metallic cigar/cylinder-like object with a line of windows or portholes sometimes visible.

4) The upturned plate. This type of UFO looks like a large dish turned upside down, so that the base appears flat and the upper part domed. Sometimes seen with lights set into the base, but often emits no light and is seen as a dark mass. At night, rotating lights are sometimes observed on the underside.

5) The Saturn shape. This type of UFO looks like the planet Saturn, a central ring separating two hemispheres. A common daylight UFO.

6) The triangle. 'Flying triangles' have become more common in recent years, but are more likely to be seen at night than day. Sometimes seen as a dark mass, sometimes with lights that define a triangular shape.

It is usually assumed that UFOs are extraterrestrial in origin, but some think the truth is even stranger. One theory holds that UFOs are psychic in nature, since encounters with UFOs and GHOSTS share a number of similar elements. For example, electromagnetic disturbances, temperature changes and night-time encounters are seen as common elements.

An even more frightening proposition is that

UFOs are 'demonic' in nature, designed to lead mankind astray through confusion and misinformation. This seemed to be the conclusion that late Welsh UFO investigator Randall Jones Pugh came to after many years of investigation. Pugh had been involved in the case of the 'Dyfed Enigma' (see below), and later concluded that UFOs were linked to the occult and that the study of UFOs was inherently dangerous.

Many UFOs are thought to be caused by geomagnetic disturbances and have been termed EARTH LIGHTS.

Wales is no stranger to UFO 'flaps', and our UFOs seem to have a penchant for lonely spots in the Welsh countryside – isolated rural roads and settlements as well as the mountain regions.

There seems to be some evidence for a peak in activity every ten years (at least in Wales). If we take 1977 as a starting point, this was the year of the world-famous 'Dyfed Enigma'. An area between Haverfordwest, St David's and St Brides became known as the 'Welsh Triangle', a WINDOW AREA where strange occurrences included cars pursued by 'orange footballs', 'glowing cigars' and 'disks flying into solid rock and vanishing between sliding doors' (Stack Rocks). 'Giant faceless humanoids' peered in through the windows of a farm and 'sinister aliens with psychic powers' plagued locals. If this weren't enough, a herd of cows was seemingly

'teleported' and strange sights became almost commonplace.

Much of the activity seemed to be focused on the Coombs family of Ripperston Farm, near St Brides Bay. Many of the events experienced by the family, such as teleportation and electromagnetic disturbances, lead some to draw parallels with poltergeist phenomena.

A number of Welsh regions saw an increase in UFO activity in 1987. 'Flying triangles' and 'strobe lights' were seen in and around Hafren Forest, and then 1997 saw a 'flap' in North Wales with multiple sightings on the Great Orme (see *Lonely Moors and Sinister Hills*).

WEREWOLF: A werewolf is a person who shapeshifts into a wolf or wolf-like creature. This is usuallly the result of purposeful magic or a curse. The trasnformation is said to occur during a full moon. See also BLACK DOGS and ALIEN BIG CATS.

WILD HUNT : See CWN ANNWN.

WILL-O'-THE-WISP: Also known as *Ignis fatuus* or 'Fool's Fire'. See SPOOK LIGHT and CORPSE CANDLE.

WINDOW AREA: A window area is a region with an unusually high number of paranormal and/or UFO reports. Some feel that phenomena observed in window areas are somehow related to geomagnetic disturbances

The High Mountains

I saw them – the mighty of ages departed – The dead were around me that night on the hill: From their eyes, as they pass'd, a cold radiance they darted. There was light on my soul, but my heart's blood was chill. (From Felicia Heman's *The Rock of Cader Idris*)

Mount Olympus, home of the Greek gods, Mount Fuji, Ararat, Sinai and Everest – all well-known sacred mountains, symbols of veneration and awe throughout history. You could be forgiven for thinking that sacred mountains are the preserve of 'exotic' countries. However, a modest amount of research will reveal that there are many such mountains in the British Isles.

Wales, land of mountains, has more than its fair share of Britain's sacred high places. History, culture and folklore are inextricably linked to landscapes, and, to our ancestors, the untamed uplands were home to strange creatures and ethereal supernatural beings. They were places to be avoided and revered from afar, the stuff of folk memory, fireside stories passed from generation to generation.

Vast, brooding and occasionally deadly, mountains can be rather frightening places. The weather in the Welsh uplands is famously fickle and conditions can change very quickly. Snow, rain, mists and low cloud are some of the well-known mountain hazards. For the unprepared, the slippery knife-edge ridges of a remote mountain are genuine threats to life. It would not be surprising if such dangers were associated with supernatural agencies in times past.

It follows that the rational mind might dismiss the stories of old as mere manifestations of legitimate fears, but now and again a contemporary mystery comes to light. A popular theory suggests that a great deal of unexplained phenomena is extremely ancient and has been interpreted in different ways at different times. The Berwyn Mountains 'UFO Incident' is a good example. Strange lights and 'dragons' have been seen in the area for hundreds of years, and the incident described in this book would have been interpreted very differently by previous generations (even if the lights represented a 'genuine' UFO).

Could an unexplained elemental power be responsible for the multitude of strange lights, ghostly entities and supernatural creatures said to inhabit certain Welsh mountain regions? Are the veils between worlds thin on certain mountains? Whatever the answers, it seems that, for now, the mysteries endure, which is good news for the supernatural explorer.

Snowdon Frighteners

We begin our journey high on the jagged peaks of Snowdonia, north Wales. Covering an area of 2,171 square kilometres (838 square miles), Snowdonia National Park takes its English name from Mount Snowdon. In Welsh the park is called Eryri, which means 'place of the eagles'.

The remains of a long-extinct volcano, Snowdon (Yr Wyddfa) is the highest mountain in Wales and the highest British mountain south of the Scottish Highlands, reaching an altitude of 1,085m (3,560ft). At the centre of the extensive Snowdon massif is Yr Wyddfa itself, the peak commonly referred to as Snowdon.

The English name Snowdon comes from the Saxon words 'Snow Dun', meaning 'snow hill', but in old Welsh Yr Wyfdda means 'the grave'. Legend suggests that a huge stone cairn near the top of the mountain once marked the grave of the giant Ricca, better known as Rhita. It seems Rhita was particularly fierce, as he had a cloak made out of the beards of all the kings he'd killed. King Arthur is said to have slain Rhita and won his cloak.

It comes as little surprise that Wales's greatest and most famous mountain is the setting for a number of sinister tales. The Brenin Llwyd (Welsh for 'Grey King' or 'Monarch of the Mist') is a being believed by some to inhabit Snowdon and its ranges. Reports of its appearance vary. Sometimes, the Brenin Llwyd is felt as a presence, and sometimes it takes on a physical form like the American Bigfoot or Himalayan Yeti. It seems to be an entity/creature of a class similar to

The sinister black cliffs of Clogwen Du'r Arddu, Snowdon

the Am Fear Liath Môr or 'Big Grey Man' of Ben Macdui, Scotland. Note that the Am Fear Liath Môr is also known as the 'Greyman'.

The Scottish man-beast is said to cause feelings of terror in those who climb Britain's second-highest mountain. In 1925 the climber John Norman Collie was 'seized with terror' after hearing the crunch of unseen feet following him. Many who claim to have encountered the American Bigfoot have reported similarly powerful feelings of terror and panic.

It is said that the mountain guides of old were extremely wary of the Brenin Llwyd, who, according to folklorist Marie Trevelyan, is said to 'travel stealthily and silently up through the ravines' or 'sit waiting among lonely peaks to seize and imprison the unwary'.

Intriguingly, weird creatures resembling a man-beast or Bigfoot have been spotted in Snowdonia fairly recently. In response to a number of reports from members of the public, a forester and a group of friends are said to have mounted an expedition into the mountains to locate a 'monstrous beast'. One night the beast attacked the expedition camp, allowing the party to get a good look at the creature. In common with other British man-beasts, it was reported as being about ten feet tall with huge hands, was covered in dark brown hair and had red eyes.

Llyn Du'r Arddu (The Black Lake of Arddu) is surely the most sinister place on Snowdon. Arddu (more correctly spelt *Aredig*) means plough, though some associate the word with a 'dark one/lord' – a supernatural personification of death similar to the much-feared Ankou of Breton folklore. Above the lake, the towering black cliffs of Clogwen Du'r Arddu loom threateningly and contribute greatly to the eerie atmosphere.

The area is very popular for 'wild camping,' but spending a night at the demon-haunted Maen Du'r Arddu (Black Stone of Arddu) could cost you dear. Folklore dictates that you will wake a poet, a madman or dead. Should you spend a night near the lake you will find that the area exudes dark magic and mystery. It is said that fairies and goblins dance on the shores and that the spot is haunted – perhaps by the Brenin Llwyd himself.

Goblins, and perhaps the Brenin Llwyd himself, haunt Llyn Du'r Arddu

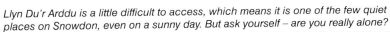

Llyn Du'r Arddu is a little difficult to access, which means it is one of the few quiet places on Snowdon, even on a sunny day. But ask yourself – are you really alone?

Walk 1 – Llyn Du'r Arddu

WALK INFORMATION:
START: Snowdon Mountain Railway Station GR SH582597
PARKING: Opposite station/Llanberis
RECOMMENDED MAP: OS Explorer OL17 or Landranger 115
DISTANCE (APPROX): 11km / 7 miles
TIME (APPROX): 4 hours
WALK TYPE: Linear
DIFFICULTY RATING: Energetic
NOTES: The steep and bouldery descent to Llyn Du'r Arddu should be avoided in poor weather.

1. With your back to the Snowdon Mountain Railway station, turn right and take the first right up Victoria Terrace – at the junction there is a sign saying 'Footpath up Snowdon'. Follow the road to an interpretation board and cattle grid. Continue up a steep metalled track, through a gate to a fingerpost on the left indicating 'To Snowdon'. Turn left through the gate to follow a well-defined rough track gently uphill. Cross a ladder stile next to a gate and continue up along the path, which runs parallel to the railway for a while. Eventually the path runs underneath the railway line and continues uphill to Halfway House at 500m (1,700 ft).

2. From Halfway House continue up to a point where the Llanberis Path starts to bend to the left and ascend steeply. Look out for a fairly level grassy path continuing straight on away from the Llanberis Path towards the cliffs of Clogwen Du'r Arddu. Pass a ruined building on the left and approximately 30m further on you will reach a small rocky stream and several boulders to your left.

3. At this point you can scramble down to the lake below (be warned – only attempt this if you have experience of walking in steep terrain). Facing downhill move to the left of the stream (opposite the last big boulder) and very carefully make your way downhill, rejoining the stream after a few metres (this avoids a steep section

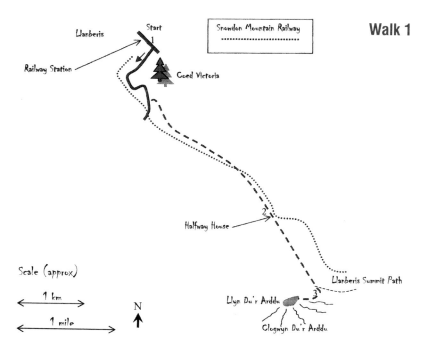

where the stream joins the path). Follow the stream down to the lake. Remember, although the stream was a mere trickle when I visited, during wet periods it would be advisable to avoid the 'final descent' or navigate to the lake using an alternative route.

The Haunted Mountain Pass

The beautiful Pass of Aberglaslyn lies a few miles to the south of Snowdon, near the famous village of Beddgelert. This mountainous wooded gorge is reminiscent of an Alpine scene, with sheer 700ft cliffs towering either side of the River Glaslyn, surrounded on all sides by mighty mountains.

The area is associated with 'the little people' (seen playing in the river by a Mr William Jones in the nineteenth century) and, of course, the 'tourist' legend of the unfortunate hound Gelert, who was supposed to have been accidentally killed by his master after saving the master's young child from a wolf.

Although the Pass of Aberglaslyn is a well-known Snowdonia tourist destination by day, it seems that at night it takes on a more sinister aspect. The pass represents a rare break in a mercilessly mountainous landscape, and travellers have had to brave a night-time journey on more than one occasion.

On a bright sunny the day the pass is a place of great natural beauty and seems far from sinister, but make no mistake, this is one of Wales's most haunted places. On an evening stroll the atmosphere inevitably changes, and a number of disturbing phenomena could be encountered. A large Black Dog haunts the pass, as do a phantom horseman, strange lights and a ghostly white lady. The white lady should be avoided if possible, as she is said to be a harbinger of death and misfortune.

Walk 2 – Aberglaslyn Pass

WALK INFORMATION:
START/PARKING: National Trust car park, Nantmor (pay and display) GR SH597462
RECOMMENDED MAP: OS Explorer OL17 or Landranger 115
DISTANCE (APPROX): 7.5km / 4.5 miles
TIME (APPROX): 2.5 hours
WALK TYPE: Circular
DIFFICULTY RATING: Moderate
NOTES: The Welsh Highland Railway is to be re-opened and may result in modifications that affect the route. Start from Beddgelert and avoid the Nantmor section in poor weather/light.

1. From the National Trust car park at Nantmor, go through the gate to the left of the building and cross a stone stile. Go up through a gate between stone walls and pass by an old stone cottage on the left as you walk through a wood. The 'Fisherman's Path' (as it is known) becomes increasingly rocky and veers right near a kissing gate (leading onto the road near the bridge on your left). As you enter the pass, be aware that the path can be dangerous due to high drops down to the river on your left.

2. Continue on along the narrow rocky path, passing a number of walkways and steps en route. At first, the path is rather adventurous and undulates dramatically, but eventually it levels out and becomes a pleasant gravel track with the Welsh Highland Railway to your right. Pass an interpretation board within a walled enclosure and cross the railway via two gates. Pass a bridge across the river to your left (you will cross this on your return journey) and cross the railway via two more gates. Go through a gate between two walls and pass a hotel on the right. Go through an ornate wooden gate near a footbridge across the river just before you enter Beddgelert town, cross the bridge and turn left on the other side of the river to go through a gate signposted 'Gelert's Grave'.

3. Follow a metalled path, taking a short circular diversion to Gelert's grave should you wish (once said to be haunted by David Prichard – originator of the story). Continue with the river to your left, passing through several more gates to reach a footbridge over to the other side of the river. Cross the bridge and turn right to re-cross the railway, and then turn left to continue with the railway to your left and the river to your right. Again you will need to take care due to the steep drops (now to your right). Eventually, you will see the stone road bridge and the kissing gate

When night falls in the mountains, the atmosphere in the Pass of Aberglaslyn changes

A host of spectral entities haunt the pass – all of them frightening

Walk 2

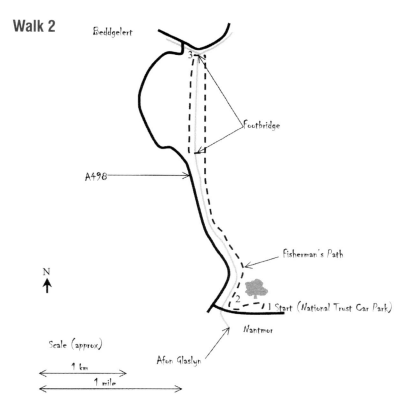

leading onto the road. Veer left and walk up the steps, following a fence on your right back through the wood. Go through a gate to the left of the old stone cottage. Follow the signs to the car park – reached via the stone stile and gate.

If you fancy an evening walk, you should undertake this walk from the Beddgelert side (3), passing by Gelert's grave and turning left back towards Beddgelert after crossing the bridge over the river. This avoids the steep and potentially hazardous Nantmor section of the Fisherman's Path.

The Supernatural Mountain

In the southern part of Snowdonia National Park, near Dolgellau, rises the 'mighty rock' of Cadair Idris. The mountain looms primeval over the Mawddach Estuary, and is considered by some to be a greater mountain than Snowdon.

Although smaller than Snowdon at 2,927 feet (892 metres), Cadair Idris feels much bigger, and was once thought to be the highest peak in Wales. The mountain consists of a wild and exposed 11km (7-mile) long ridge, the northern part of which is very steep and rocky. In general, the southern end slopes off more gently. The main summit (one of three peaks on the ridge) is called Penygadair (Peak of the Chair). The

25

The Minfordd Path up Cadair Idris, Wales's most supernatural mountain

mountain is mainly composed of Ordovician igneous (volcanic) rock and bears the scars of classic glacial erosion. One long-held belief was that Cadair Idris represents the remains of huge conical volcano. However, although much of the rock is volcanic in origin, the crater-like Llyn Cau is actually a deep glacial corrie lake or tarn.

Well known for its arctic-alpine plants and upland heath, the area is (according to the Countryside Council for Wales) of 'outstanding geomorphological importance including features such as the extensive Talyllyn fault, several corries and narrow summit ridges'. However, many claim that the mountain is special for other, stranger reasons. No other mountain in Wales (perhaps in the whole of Britain) has attracted as much lore as Cadair Idris. Many intuitively feel that this is a sacred, magical place.

The name 'Cadair Idris' means 'Chair of Idris' – a shadowy figure of the Welsh Dark Ages, sometimes associated with King Arthur. The 'chair' is thought by some to be a reference to the armchair-like shape of Cwm Gadair, although it could relate to a number of 'armchair'-like landforms on the mountain.

The mountain is said to be a 'gateway' to the Underworld. It is frequently referred to as a haunt of 'troops' of fairies, as well as the much-feared Cŵn Annwn – terrifying Hell Hounds belonging to Arawn, king of the Underworld. Llyn Cau is said to be bottomless and is the abode of a man-eating monster. It certainly has an eerie quality – and is known to be an incredible 50m (165ft) in depth. Once, a swimmer foolishly swam across the lake and was taken under the water, never to be seen again.

As with Mae Du'r Arddu on Snowdon, those spending a night on the summit will wake a poet, a madman or dead. To the present day the summit and nearby stone shelter are said to be supernaturally 'active' and spending the night can be an extremely unnerving experience.

Many people complain of feelings of being watched on the hill. This isn't surprising as Cadair Idris is another favoured haunt of the Brenin Llwyd. Susan Cooper's novel *The Grey King*, the fourth book in *The Dark is Rising* series, is named after the Welsh mountain entity. In the book, the Grey King is a powerful 'dark lord' – a dangerous ever-present and oppressive force around the mountain.

Perhaps due to the proximity of geological faults, this is one of the best places in Wales to see 'earth lights' or 'spook lights'. Like the Berwyns, Cadair Idris is said to be an abode of dragons – in the next story I suggest there is a connection between earth lights and dragon folklore. The lights are supposed to be visible near the peak on the first night of the Celtic New Year or the first night of the New Year (1 November or 1 January). Some maintain that the lights are a manifestation of fairies that leave the mountain at certain times of the year.

The lights were observed by earth light researcher Paul Devereux on one of the three 'spirit nights' – Midsummer's Eve, 23 June). Devereux and a number of witnesses observed 'A blue-white light erupt from the north side of the mountain'. It was estimated to be travelling at 600mph. This adds a new dimension to a well-known version of the famous song, *Men of Harlech* – 'Tongues of fire on Idris flaring...'

In January 2007 it seems the lights returned to the region. Multiple witnesses saw a blue-green light streaking across Cardigan Bay. It was estimated as being at least 50 times larger than a shooting star.

Walk 3 – Cadair Idris

WALK INFORMATION:
START/PARKING: Dôl Idris car park next to Minfordd Hotel GR SH732115
RECOMMENDED MAP: OS Explorer OL23 or Landranger 124
DISTANCE (APPROX): 4km / 2.5 miles
TIME (APPROX): 2 to 2.5 hours
WALK TYPE: Linear
DIFFICULTY RATING: Energetic
NOTES: Summit walks should only be attempted by fully equipped and experienced hill-walkers.

There are a number of summit routes up Cadair Idris, and a myriad of walking guides describe the routes. This linear walk is more suitable for those who seek to witness earth lights and experience the mystery and power of the mountain at times when there are few people around. To this end, it is a relatively 'safe' route compared

Llyn Cau is a good place to watch for earth lights, but beware – the lake is home to a man-eating monster

Walk 3

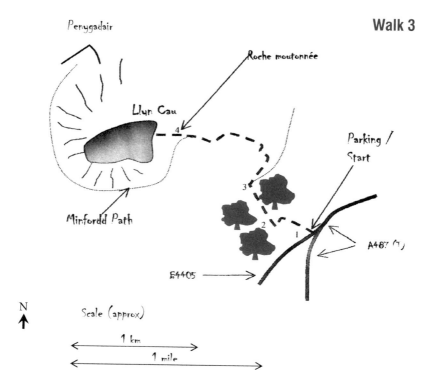

to the summit routes (as long as you don't stray from the path), and the walk shouldn't leave you completely exhausted!

1. At the end of the car park go through a gate to follow a track, crossing a bridge to reach a kissing gate. Go through the kissing gate and pass the cottage to reach a gate that leads into the nature reserve and a prominent waymarker indicating 'Cadair Idris'.

2. Follow the steep path up through the ancient oak woods with the stream on your right. Much of the time you will find yourself ascending steps of varying kinds. Take time to enjoy the woodlands, which are a reminiscent of the 'wildwood' (See *Haunted Woods and Wooded Lanes*).

3. After a fairly steep climb you will reach a gate leading to more open country. Go through the gate and continue to a waymarker post with

conifer plantations on your right. Continue straight on in the direction of 'Cwm Cau'. The path off to the right leads to Mynydd Moel and eventually reaches Penygadair. Pass some ruined buildings on the left and follow the path as it ascends and veers around to the left, then around to the right under a section of steep ground to your left. In certain places the path becomes rocky and a little difficult to follow. Continue on to a huge tear-shaped rock, ignoring the Minfordd Path as it veers left towards the top of the ridge.

4. The huge rock is a roche moutonnée, a chunk of bedrock that has been subjected to glacial scouring – note the lines on the surface of the rock, which are known as glacial striations or glacial grooves. These were formed when the gravel and boulders in the base of a moving glacier ground against the rock during the last Ice Age, the peak of which occurred around

18,000 years ago. Pass to the left of the roche moutonnée and continue straight on along fairly level ground to reach Llyn Cau.

The Berwyn Mountains UFO-Dragon

It is said that Uther Pendragon, the father of King Arthur, adopted the Celtic red dragon as a standard after seeing a vision of a flaming dragon in the sky. Could the sky dragons of yesteryear be the UFOs of modern times? Could UFOs be associated with geological faults and the strange phenomena known as earth lights?

The Berwyn Mountains, bounded to the north and west by the Bala Fault, are a place where the distinctions between myth, legend and reality become blurred. Lying outside the boundaries of Snowdonia National Park, this area is (or was until recently) a forgotten gem. This is an area of high moors and steep valleys running north-east across central Wales, separating Shropshire from Snowdonia, mid-Wales from north. The area is famous for its deep heather and vast moors. The high tops lie along a spectacular 2km-long ridge running roughly north to south. Cadair Berwyn (chair of the white tops) is the highest peak at

2723ft (830m). The name probably came about because of the amount of snow these relatively cold, inland hills can get in the winter.

This is an ancient landscape. Rhos y Beddau (Moor of the Graves) includes a Bronze Age stone avenue and attests to the spiritual importance of these uplands. In the distant past, these rugged hills were a known haunt of all manner of weird phenomena. Craig Rhiwarth hill fort was dreaded because of its wicked fairies, a giant roamed the hills and the Cŵn Annwn patrolled the skies. But worst of all, this was dragon country.

Dragons could be encountered amongst the mountain ravines, and were said to have caused devastation in and around the remote village of Maes Mochnant. Here, the villagers tricked a dragon into impaling itself on iron spikes attached to the Maes Mochant standing stone. The stone was draped in red cloth to infuriate and attract the dragon. Similarly, the nearby village of Penygarnedd and surrounding areas were once 'infested' with dragons.

This sets the scene for a strange and controversial case that became known as the Berwyn Mountains UFO Incident. On the evening of 23 January 1974, thousands of people reported

Scene of a UFO crash? Moel Ty Uchaf cairn circle and the high Berwyns

B4391 mountain road: the scene of a close encounter with a UFO – or was it a dragon?

a number of loud explosions followed by an earthquake measuring between 3.5 and 4 on the Richter Scale, recorded at 8.38pm by the former Geological Sciences Institute in Edinburgh. The main activity seemed to be focused on the mountains immediately surrounding Llandrillo (Clwyd), in particular the ridge that includes Moel Sych, Cadair Berwyn and Cadair Bronwen.

As one would expect, many people rushed outside to see what was going on. Before and after the event, yellow and blue lights (one with a fiery tail) were seen in the sky, and a strange glow was seen on the mountains. A large, glowing 'something' was seen to fall into the mountains, and this seemed to coincide with the earth tremor. A meteorite impact or a plane crash was initially thought to be the cause, but this theory was later discounted.

Fearing a plane crash, a local nurse drove up into the mountains along the B4391 mountain road with her two daughters in tow. At the point the road levels out she saw a large circular object, which emitted glowing colours, as well as a number of smaller lights.

Later, anomalous high radiation readings were obtained from Moel Ty Uchaf – a famously

perfect early Bronze Age cairn circle.

It seems that a later incident involving a downed military jet, exaggeration and misinterpretation of events sowed the seeds of confusion. Stories of 'Men in Black' and shadowy military activity have distorted the nature of what is perhaps a mysterious, ancient phenomenon related to those seen around Cadair Idris – the Berwyn mountains 'dragon lights'.

This is a highly controversial case, but the overwhelming evidence leads one to conclude that something very strange happened that night. A few reports suggest the lights have been seen since the main 'incident'. Their true nature remains a mystery to this day.

Walk 4 – Moel Ty Uchaf and the Berwyns

WALK INFORMATION:
START/PARKING: Next to river bridge, Llandrillo GR SJ035371
RECOMMENDED MAP: OS Explorer 255 or Landranger 125
DISTANCE (APPROX): 6km / 3.8 miles
TIME (APPROX): 1.5 to 2 hours
WALK TYPE: Part circular

Moel Ty Uchaf: Anomalous high radiation readings at the time of the incident

DIFFICULTY RATING: Moderate
NOTES: Navigation skills may be required in poor visibility.

1. Come out of the car park, cross the road and turn left to reach a stone cross on the right. Continue down the lane with the 'dead end' sign near the cross. Follow the lane, which becomes quite steep and bends around to the left and pass a stile and gate on the left. Continue straight up to go through a gate onto a 'green lane'.

2. Continue along this pleasant track, passing a farmhouse on your left. Go through a gate to reach a waymarker post where the track bends around to the right. Continue straight on at this point (don't follow the track around to the right). Continue along the well-worn track, go through a gate and ford a stream. Go through two more gates and ford a second stream to continue in the direction of a small copse of conifers. Immediately after the next gate turn right at a 'crossroads'.

3. Continue uphill to go through a gate. You will see conifer plantations ahead and to the right. At the corner of the fence on your right

(where it veers right with the track – if you reach another gate you've gone too far), turn left up the slope to reach Moel Ty Uchaf cairn circle – the perfect vantage place for dragon-spotting.

4. Make your way back to the track. If you want a longer walk, the well-defined track continues to a gate adjacent to the conifers and on to the high Berwyns. To return, turn right back down the track, remembering to turn left through a gate at the 'crossroads' to return to the village.

Witch Lakes of the Beacons

At 2,907 feet (886m), Pen y Fan is the highest mountain in the Brecon Beacons, and is the highest point in the British Isles south of Cadair Idris. Together with Corn Du, this mountain forms one of the most prominent and spectacular sights in South Wales

Below the steep sides of Pen y Fan and Corn Du is a small circular lake called Llyn Cwm Llwch, a lake that is reputed to mark the location of a gateway to the Underworld. In *The Welsh Fairy Book*, W Jenkyn Thomas explains that 'At the foot of Pen y Fan, the principal peak of the Beacons of Brecon, is a lake called Llyn Cwm

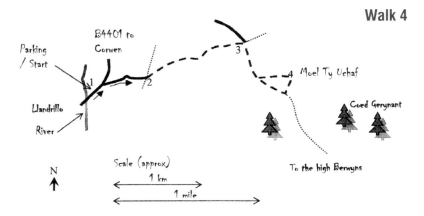

Walk 4

Llwch, overhung by frowning precipices, the home of croaking ravens, the only birds which will venture near the dark waters of the mere. In very ancient times there was a door in a rock hard by, which opened once in each year – on May Day – and disclosed a passage leading to a small island in the centre of the lake.'

The lake was once the lair of an immortal Druid witch of terrible power. She is said to have required 900 lives in order to become mortal. She preyed on the weak-willed, luring them to their death in the dark mountain waters. Perhaps she still does.

The western areas of the national park are less visited than the central Beacons, and it is beneath an area of the Black Mountain known as Bannau Sir Gaer that one finds two mysterious lakes: Llyn y Fan Fawr and Llyn y Fan Fach (the big and little Fans). Llyn y Fan Fawr was once considered sacred – votive offerings from the late Bronze Age and early Iron Age were found here in the early 1900s.

Llyn Cwm Llwch – the haunt of an 'immortal Druid witch'

The wild and remote Bannau Sir Gaer (750m) seen from below Llyn y Fan Fach. Photo Credit: Ingrid Nicholas

Both of these lakes lie in dramatic mountain amphitheatres, but it is Llyn Fan Fach that is attributed with the most enduring folklore. Llyn y Fan Fach is the lake that gave birth to the Arthurian legend of the lady in the lake. In the twelfth century, a local farmer is said to have married one of three women who emerged from the water, their offspring becoming the famous healers, the 'Physicians of Mydfai'.

Up until the nineteenth century, huge crowds of people would visit the lake on the first Sunday of August to see the emergence of the 'water nymph', whose presence was heralded by a 'commotion' in the water. An astonishing number of stories relate to the lake 'entity.' Once, a man decided to find the lake nymph. He drained the water in the lake by cutting into the bank, but encountered a 'huge hairy monster of hideous

Lyn y Fan Fach: Ancient abode of the Wives of the Underworld, hideous monsters and gigantic 8ft-long eels. One was recently reported by a water engineer and was the 'circumference of a saucer'.

aspect'. Wirt Sikes described these entities as the 'Gwragedd Annwn' – Wives of the Underworld. Presumably the lake entity still appears on the first Sunday of August. Dare you make her acquaintance?

Walk 5 – Llyn Cwm Llwch

WALK INFORMATION:
START/PARKING: SO 005244 (about a mile south-east of Libanus)
RECOMMENDED MAP: OS Explorer OL12 or Landranger 160
DISTANCE (APPROX): 6km / 3.8 miles
TIME (APPROX): 2 hours
WALK TYPE: Linear
DIFFICULTY RATING: Moderate
NOTES: The route leading up the ridge near the cairn will take you up onto the high beacons.
1. From the car park (an idyllic spot amongst oak woodland), continue straight on down a track past a 'No Motors' sign. Continue along a rocky path, cross a bridge and a stile and continue on with the stream to your left. The track continues between stone walls. Bear right just before a gate to follow a waymarker around a cottage, then left to another waymarker and straight on to a stile. Cross the stile, pass a gate on the left and shortly after cross another stile. After the stile, bear right up the path. The ascent is gentle at this stage. The path continues between scattered trees, disappears for a short distance with some banks and ditches to the right, and then ascends steeply to a large stone before a stile. Cross the stile onto National Trust-owned land (Cwm Llwch). Head straight up the hill along a well-worn steep path. As you head up towards the ridge, bear left off the main path at a large cairn (pile of stones).

Walk 5

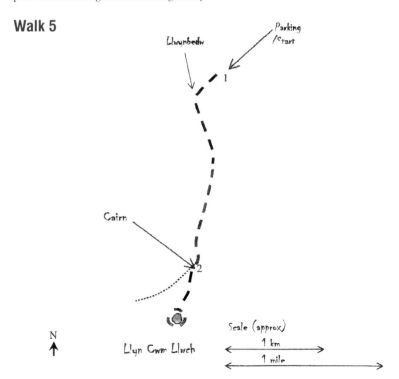

N

Scale (approx)
1 km
1 mile

2. Continue along a fairly level grassy track. The track becomes quite rocky and descends into a small stream valley, then ascends again with a rocky stream to the left. The track then levels out and leads to the lake. A walk around the lake perimeter is fairly straightforward.

Walk 6 – Llyn y Fan Fach

WALK INFORMATION:
START/PARKING: Ample off-road parking about a mile from Llanddeusant GR SN790242
RECOMMENDED MAP: OS Explorer OL12 or Landranger 160
DISTANCE (APPROX): 6km / 3.8 miles
TIME (APPROX): 1.5 to 2 hours
WALK TYPE: Linear
DIFFICULTY RATING: Moderate
NOTES: Follow signs from the Cross Inn, north of Llanddeusant.

1. From the car parking area, follow the path uphill until you reach some buildings (a trout hatchery), which you must bypass. Turn left through a wall as indicated by a sign and then turn right to follow a path to the left of the road.

2. The path rejoins the road and continues uphill, crossing a bridge on the way to reach a point where a grassy path branches off to the left. Take this left turn to follow a clockwise loop up to the lake, passing a small hut on the way.

You can walk around much of the lake but the southern side of the lake is less bouldery (keep out of the wet peaty areas). I recently found a Mesolithic flint scraper on the eastern side of the lake. The remains of ancient trees can be seen in the peat on the southern side. The hut provides a useful reference point on your return journey.

Walk 6

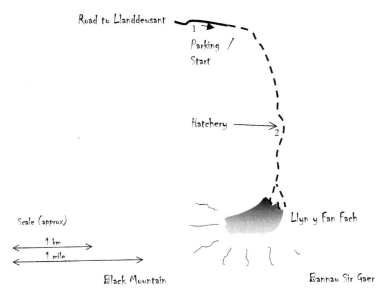

Further Exploration

More Mountain Ghosts and High Strangeness

There can be little doubt that there are many strange mountain stories to be told. Here are few more 'fireside tales'.

The 'Ghost Bear' of the Glyders

I have heard vague rumours about a 'ghost bear' that haunts the menacing ridge of Tryfan in Snowdonia. I believe the story stems from an account by Showell Styles in *The Mountains of North Wales*. The sighting took place on Bwlch y Ddwy Glyder, the saddle between the peaks of Glyder Fawr and Glyder Fach, just to the south-west of Tryfan.

Styles describes being just above the saddle on an extremely hot day. He thought he could see a fellow walker coming up the slope to the south, but then saw the shape was too big to be a human and was moving rapidly up a scree slope. Although it was the shape of a bear, the 'thing' was transparent. The 'ghost' was six or seven feet in diameter and composed of rapidly whirling dry grass. The rest of the ridge was 'utterly windless'.

Of course, this sounds very like a description of a 'dust devil'. They tend to form on very hot windless days, when surface air rises through a pocket of cooler air above it. In the right conditions, the air will begin to rotate.

The 'Roman Steps' of Rhinog Fawr

The Rhinogydd range of mountains (known in English as the Rhinogs) can be found east of Harlech in North Wales. This is a wild and 'forgotten' area that is far less visited that the 'honeypots' of Snowdonia.

A ghostly group of Roman soldiers or medieval drovers with pack animals are said to make their way up the 'Roman Steps' on Rhinog Fawr. In *Modern Mysteries of Britain*, Janet and Colin Bord describe an intriguing encounter with a ghost on the steps. The story concerns a certain Redfern Thomas and his son, and the event took place in the late 1920s. Having climbed the steps, they found the mountain deserted. The pair then suddenly became aware of a young girl. She was nicely dressed, and she approached the pair and greeted them in Welsh. Mr Thomas replied, and the girl vanished into thin air. They searched the mountain, but found nothing.

The Pumlumon Wilds

Pumlumon (or Plynlimon in its anglicised form) means 'five summits'. It is a mountain massif that rises to the highest point in the Cambrian Mountains. Pen Pumlumon Fawr – the highest peak in the range – rises to 2,467 feet (752m). The A44 from Rhayader to Aberystwyth marks the southern boundary of the range, whilst to the west lie the Afon Rheidol and Nant-y-moch reservoirs. To the east lie the vast plantations of Hafren Forest.

In legend, Pen Pumlumon Fawr was the lair of a notorious robber giant called Dillus Farfawc, who was the peril of mountain travellers. He was eventually killed for his beard, which was used to make a leash for King Arthur's great hunting hound Drudwyn. In a tale from the *Mabinogion*, Dillus Farfawc's fate is sealed after he is spotted due to rising smoke from a roasting wild boar.

The mountain is supposed to be haunted by strange lights – Corpse Candles or Will-o'-the-wisps. Just below and to the west of Pumlumon is the boggy site of a bloody battle. In June 1401 Owain Glyndŵr and his army of four hundred were camped at the bottom of the Hyddgen valley when fifteen hundred English and Flemish settlers from Pembrokeshire attacked them. Owain fought back, killing 200 and making prisoners of the rest. Could this incident be related to the Corpse Candles seen in the area?

Lonely Moors and Sinister Hills

'To that providence, my sons, I hereby commend you, and I counsel you by way of caution to forbear from crossing the moor in those dark hours when the powers of evil are exalted.'

(Hugo Baskerville's document, read by Dr Mortimer in Sir Arthur Conan Doyle's *The Hound of the Baskervilles*)

What do 'the moors' mean to you? As you have chosen to read this book, images of desolation, a lonely wilderness, *The Hound of the Baskervilles* and the cult horror film *An American Werewolf in London* may well spring to mind.

The term 'moor' is a derivative of 'moorland'. 'Moor' comes from the Saxon word for marsh. In Welsh, moorland is usually called 'Waun' or 'Mynydd' (the latter is also used with reference to specific hills and mountains).

Moorland mainly refers to the unenclosed land of the British uplands. These areas support so-called 'semi-natural' habitats of blanket bog, heathland, acid grassland and marshy grassland. Our moorland vegetation developed rapidly when humans cleared the uplands of trees and used these areas for grazing many thousands of years ago.

Moorland usually develops at altitude, and Wales is famously hilly. The uplands dominate the topography, and more than a third of the land lies above the 250m contour. People have lived, worked, worshipped and died on the wild moors of Wales for at least 8,000 years, in many areas leaving behind extremely well-preserved, enigmatic remains that have largely escaped major disturbance.

Today, the moors can seem deserted and conditions hostile, but this was not always so. Soil conditions have deteriorated since the Iron Age, but when environmental and economic conditions were favourable, the uplands were hives of activity.

In certain places, echoes of the past seem to persist. A haunted moor on a lonely hill can be one of the most frightening places to be if you find yourself in the wrong place, at the wrong time...

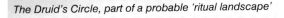

The Druid's Circle, part of a probable 'ritual landscape'

The Stone of Sacrifice

The sinister Stone of Sacrifice forms part of Y Meini Hirion, kown as 'The Druid's Circle' on the high moors south of Penmaenmawr, near Conwy on the coast of North Wales. When exploring this area with your map you will notice the astonishing range of material traces of Bronze Age culture in the landscape, leading some to speculate that this was a so-called 'ritual landscape'. Cairns, standing stones and other features abound. This was a special place.

The Druid's Circle is a visually impressive stone circle about half a mile east of Moelfre. The site was excavated between 1958 and 1959 and a number of cremation burials were discovered, including two urns containing the burnt remains of children. Constructed between 1450 and 1400 BC, the circle predates the Druids by a thousand years. We will never know who has used the site and for what purposes in the years between the circle's construction in the Bronze Age and the present. Perhaps the Druids 'adopted' the site for their own ceremonial purposes.

Two of the stones in particular have supernatural stories attached to them – the Deity Stone and the Stone of Sacrifice. The Deity Stone is said to physically punish blasphemers. One

blasphemer was said to have laughed to scorn the stone, and one night decided to test the stories. He went up to the Druid's Circle and shouted blasphemies at the top of his voice. In the morning he was found battered to death at the base of the Deity Stone.

Witches were said to have held their strange ceremonies at the circle. One night, during a ceremony, the stone began to issue 'stern maledictions'. The witches were so frightened by the venom of the curses issuing from the stone that two died and one went mad.

The Stone of Sacrifice stands immediately opposite the Deity Stone. Disturbingly, the stone has a depression in it just large enough to hold a child. On windy, stormy nights, terrible moans and sobs can be heard coming from the stone – echoes of a tragedy and terror that transcends time.

As with some other Welsh supernatural sites, UFOs and strange lights are particularly attracted to the moors immediately surrounding the Druid's Circle. A high number of UFOs have been seen on Moelfre, including bright star-like objects that suddenly changed direction and a 'giant sparkler' that had two separate 'tongues of flame' with red and yellow colours at their centre.

Ready to pounce: beware of the Deity Stone, as it has supernatural powers, can issue fatal curses and can physically punish blasphemers

Walk 7 – Moelfre and The Druid's Circle

WALK INFORMATION:
START/ PARKING: Library Car Park, Penmaenmawr GR SH719762
RECOMMENDED MAP: OS Explorer OL17 or Landranger 115
DISTANCE (APPROX): 8km / 5 miles
TIME (APPROX): 2.5 to 3 hours
WALK TYPE: Part circular
DIFFICULTY RATING: Moderate
NOTES: The initial steep climb can be quite tiring. Navigation skills may be required on the open ground between Moelfre and the Druid's Circle.

1. Turn right out of the library car park and right again onto Y Berllan. Take the first turning left then right and continue on to where the road ends. Follow a footpath between two hedges up to a caravan park on Graiglwyd Road. Turn right along the road, then at a fingerpost indicating 'Druid's Circle' turn left down a farm track and cross a stile. Pass to the left of the farm to a gate. At the gate a waymarker points to a kissing gate up a bank to the right. Go through the kissing gate and follow the well-worn path around to the left.

2. Follow the grassy track steeply uphill (take advantage of the benches along the way). Continue uphill, following the path as it zigzags right and left along a steep section. The path eventually levels out and swings around to the left to cross a concrete bridge over wet and boggy ground. Cross the bridge and go through a kissing gate towards a waymarker post indicating 'North Wales Path'.

3. Turn right along a level path with a stone wall to your right. After about 300m (300 yards), bear left over open ground to ascend the domed peak of Moelfre (navigation skills will be required in poor weather conditions). A pile of stones marks the summit.

4. From the summit, turn back with the sea to your left and descend following a poorly defined track along the ridge, veering left slightly. Pass some enigmatic stone remains before reaching the Druid's Circle itself.

5. With the sea to your left, turn left down a track to the left of the Stone of Sacrifice. Follow the poorly defined track crossing two small streams (boggy in places), to reach the North Wales Path. Turn left to reach the waymarker post you passed earlier then turn diagonally right

Terrible moans and sobs issue from the Stone of Sacrifice on dark, stormy nights. Note the depression in the top of the stone, said to have been used for dark rituals.

Walk 7   Penmaenmawr

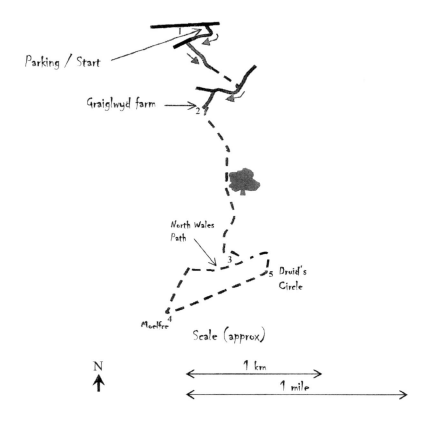

Parking / Start

Graiglwyd farm → 2

North Wales Path

3

5 Druid's Circle

Moelfre 4

Scale (approx)

N ↑

1 km

1 mile

to go back to the kissing gate. Cross the concrete bridge and turn right to return down the hill.

Through a Glass, Darkly

If you desperately want to see a UFO, experience time anomalies or perhaps get abducted by beings from another world, you will need to head for the Great Orme.

The Great Orme is a prominent limestone headland in Llandudno, on the coast of North Wales. A similar headland (Little Orme) can be found on the opposite side of the bay. The word *Orme* is said to have originally come from the

Viking *urm* or *orm*, meaning sea serpent, though there is disagreement as to the precise origins of the name.

The headland is famous for its Bronze Age copper mines – said to be amongst the world's greatest prehistoric underground excavations. Perhaps the metal ores within the limestone geology are responsible for some of the weird phenomena reported on this windswept headland – for it seems the Great Orme attracts more UFOs than anywhere else in Wales.

A survey of the most common places in Britain for UFO sightings ranked the Great Orme third out of the forty most UFO haunted

The Great Orme is the most UFO-haunted location in Wales, and the third most common place in Britain for UFO sightings

locations, after Bonnybridge in Stirlingshire and Cley Hill in Wiltshire. In November 1997 there were multiple sightings of UFOs over and near the Orme. 'Frightening' lights and weird aerial objects were seen above the headland. Time anomalies and visits by sinister 'men in black' were reported by a family en route to the Orme after they were 'buzzed' by a purple craft on the B4529 road near Bodfari. In a separate incident on the same road, a businessman saw a 'huge' flying object with numerous lit windows.

Some of the weird events described by a family en route to the Orme have parallels with many other 'UFO' encounters, with elements commonly described as the 'Oz Factor'. The term was coined by ufologist Jenny Randles and popularised by her 1983 book, *UFO Reality*. Randles defined the Oz Factor as 'the sensation of being isolated, or transported from the real world into a different environmental framework … where reality is but slightly different, [as in] the fairytale land of Oz'. In *Time Storms*, Randles puts forward a case for 'holes in time' as a result of a strange unexplained phenomenon.

It's an interesting thought. Could certain lonely places in our charming, seemingly benign Welsh countryside be conduits for forces capable of tearing apart the very fabric of our reality

– the space–time continuum itself? The records show that 1987 was a 'good year' for UFOs in Wales. Multiple sightings occurred over the Great Orme and surrounding areas in 1997, and it's said that the phenomenon peaks every ten years. So be prepared for more 'time storms' in 2007 and 2014…

Walk 8 – Great Orme

WALK INFORMATION:
START/PARKING: Great Orme Country Park Visitor Centre GR SH765833
RECOMMENDED MAP: OS Explorer OL17 or Landranger 115
DISTANCE (APPROX): 3km / 2 miles
TIME (APPROX): 1 hour
WALK TYPE: Circular
DIFFICULTY RATING: Easy
NOTES: The drystone walls provide a useful 'handrail' making this walk very easy to follow.

1. From the car park, walk back through the main entrance. Follow the road down for a short distance towards a quarry on the right. Follow a track right, passing the quarry on the left to reach the corner of a stone wall. Ignore

41

Walk 8

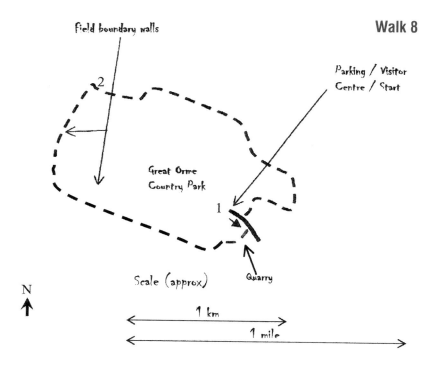

Field boundary walls

2

Parking / Visitor
Centre / Start

Great Orme
Country Park

1

Quarry

N

Scale (approx)

1 km

1 mile

The mysterious Great Orme makes an excellent elevated UFO viewing platform

a waymarker pointing left and turn right to follow the line of the wall and continue straight on. Follow the wall as it bends to the right with a cairn to the left. Continue to the next corner of the wall.

2. Near this point on your left are some 'glacial erratics' – stones left in the landscape from the last Ice Age. Some of the stones have names (the Mother and Daughter Stones, for example). For some reason, many people have reported feeling 'uneasy' in this area, particularly after dark. From the corner of the wall (facing the sea), turn right to walk back in the direction of the visitor centre with the sea now to your left and the wall to your right. Follow the line of the wall as it bulges out to the left then right – the track becomes extremely well-defined and eventually leaves the walls. Continue on to a wamarker post near the point where the track joins a metalled road and bear right, following the waymarkers uphill and back to the car park.

Mysteries of the Moels

The Clwydian Range of hills in north-east Wales seem to be a 'hotbed' of UFO and earth light activity. Indeed, so many strange lights are reported in this region that it could be described as a 'window area' (see *Supernatural History*).

This 35km/22 mile-long range of hills stretches from the Vale of Clwyd in the west to the foothills of the Dee Estuary to the east, and from Prestatyn Hillside in the north to the Nant y Garth pass in the South.

Numerous hill forts are to be found throughout the range, including Moel Arthur – the setting for a number of old stories about encounters with ghosts and strange lights.

According to folklorist Marie Trevelyan, 'A woman robed in grey formerly used to frequent a spot on Moel Arthur, overlooking the Vale of Clwyd, in North Wales. Under a rock near which the grey lady was chiefly seen, treasure was concealed in an iron chest with a ring handle. People said that the place of concealment was illuminated by a supernatural light.'

The Clwydian Range: a landscape of heather, hill forts, UFOs and haunted hills

The summit of Moel Famau has recently gained attention for its 'dancing mountain ghost'. She has been seen by multiple witnesses and appears to be wearing a blue dress.

In *British Goblins*, Wirt Sikes tells us that 'several people thereabouts are known to have seen the light, and there are even men who will tell you that bold adventurers have so far succeeded as to grasp the handle of the iron chest, when an outburst of wild tempest wrested it from their hold and struck them senseless'.

This sounds similar to the ghost of Bryn yr Ellyllon (Hill of the Goblins), which once stood near Pentre. In the 1830s a farmer's wife saw lights in a nearby wood and a ghost shimmering with golden light disappear into the mound. Later a priceless Bronze Age gold cape was discovered – the famous Mold Cape, now on display in the British Museum. Could the treasure of Moel Arthur still lie undiscovered?

Nearby, Moel Famau is the scene of many UFO sightings, and has recently gained attention for its 'dancing mountain ghost' and other strange phenomena, in particular around the remains of the Jubilee Tower at the top of the hill. The ghost is described as wearing a light blue dress, and has been seen by multiple witnesses. Strange lights, sounds, dark figures and

'orbs' have also been reported.

Why the summit of this small mountain should be haunted is something of a mystery. It has been suggested that the ghost is actually a nature spirit/fairy, or perhaps a youthful 'Hag of the Mist'. It seems strange that the ghost is most often seen near to or actually on the Jubilee Tower itself.

The remains of the tower may look a bit out of place, but they represent all that is left of a once incredible sight. It was built around 1810 to commemorate the jubilee of King George III and designed by the Chester architect Thomas Harrison, who conceived the designs for a 160ft-tall (50m) Egyptian-style obelisk. Unfortunately, the tower was irreparably damaged during a storm in 1862, and after it was made safe all that remained were the lower tiers.

Who haunts the tower? I would suggest taking a walk to the top of Moel Famau and spending some time alone at the monument. After all, this is the only way you may find out for sure.

Walk 9 – Moel Famau

WALK INFORMATION:
START/PARKING: Moel Famau Country Park Car Park GR SJ161605
RECOMMENDED MAP: OS Explorer OL17 or Landranger 115
DISTANCE (APPROX): 5km / 3 miles
TIME (APPROX): 1.5 hours
WALK TYPE: Linear
DIFFICULTY RATING: Moderate
NOTES: The car park is pay and display and closes in the early evening. For evening ascents, you will need to park alongside the road. As the road is narrow and space is limited, you may have to park further down the hill in the direction of Coed Moel Famau car park. (Alternative routes can be undertaken from Coed Moel Famau car park and Loggerheads.)

This is the easiest and most direct route to the 'haunted tower' of Moel Famau. From the car park follow the route as indicted by the fingerpost that says 'Jubilee Tower 1.75 km'. At first this extremely easy to follow path is fairly gentle, but it becomes steeper with a sharp ascent at the end, close to the Jubilee Tower at the summit.

Ghosts and Monsters of Denbigh Moor

The Denbigh Moors (Mynydd Hiraethog) seem to be the focus of numerous supernatural phenomena. These bleak, deserted moorlands are situated at the northern end of the Cambrian Mountains and comprise a large upland area between the river valleys of the Clwyd and Conwy in North Wales. To the east of the moors

Walk 9

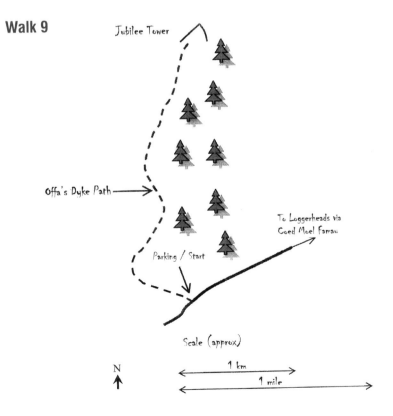

Jubilee Tower

Offa's Dyke Path

Parking / Start

To Loggerheads via Coed Moel Famau

Scale (approx)

1 km

1 mile

N

Werewolves, Black Dogs, ghosts and UFOs are said to roam the Denbigh Moors

lie the vast plantations of Clocaenog Forest (an area known for its own mysteries – Craig Bron Bannog is known for its dancing little people).

This ancient landscape is the setting for numerous ghost stories, UFO events and an encounter with a terrifying werewolf-like creature.

The most disturbing ghost story concerns the ghost of a Roman Centurion, said to be an omen of death to those who see him. The spot favoured by this spectre is rather vaguely referred to as a bridge on the road from Ruthin to Cerigydruidion (one source says about five miles from Ruthin).

The Centurion appears in full Roman military uniform – complete with helmet, breastplate and sandals. He is said to hold a short sword above his head. A number of fishermen are said to have had the unfortunate experience of seeing the ghost, and have subsequently suffered ill fortune and death. One particular group saw the Centurion on a wet and misty day after tempting fate by joking about the ghost. Suddenly, through the mist a figure began to resolve. It was the Centurion! A month later one of the party is said to have died of an alleged heart disorder.

High on the moors, near to the lonely Sportsman's Arms pub, stand the isolated ruins of Gwylfa Hiraethog – known locally as 'the haunted house'. The elaborate house was once a hunting lodge, built in 1908 by Merseyside entrepreneur Hudson Ewbanke Kearley, 1st Viscount Devonport, to accommodate shooting parties. The once-magnificent Jacobean-style lodge is now a neglected ruin, and its isolated moorland setting gives the site a sinister feel. Indeed, something 'unearthly' was seen in the ruins one night – the bizarre apparition of a tall, glowing skeleton.

I was amused by a playful reference to the nearby pub on the website of a local band called Fflint Central: 'After exploring the house in 1993, we called into the Sportsman's Arms for a pint. Just inside the door, in a glass case, was a bright red bust of Satan, complete with devilish grin, horns and pointed goatee. We never had the courage to ask the landlord its significance.' Unfortunately, I didn't have time to go inside the pub when I was researching the area, so I've no idea whether the bust is still there!

There are many other ghosts of the Hiraethog, and the moor is a well-known UFO haunt. However, even stranger things may be encountered. Further on in this section, you will read about the location used in the film, *An American Werewolf in London*. In fact, the Denbigh Moors

A bad place to fish. Could this bridge be the haunt of a Roman death-omen?

Something 'unearthly' haunts Gwylfa Hiraethog – 'the haunted house'

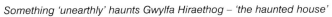

might have been a more accurate location for a moon-loving lycanthrope. However, 'staying on the road' and 'keeping off the moor' may not help in this instance.

According to author Tom Slemen, a savage werewolf roamed the Denbigh Moors in the late 1700s. At the time of the appearance of the werewolf, locals whispered about a 'bad moon on the rise' due to its strange red colour. The red colour was possibly a result of forest fires at the time, but a total eclipse can have the same effect. On 3 March 2007 the moon turned red across Britain due such an eclipse. 'Blood moons', as they were known , were greatly feared.

One full-moon night the werewolf attacked and overturned a coach travelling between Denbigh and Wrexham. The beast was said to have been the size of a donkey. The following year, it seems an 'enormous black beast' caused death and mutilation to livestock and killed a farm dog before terrorising a farmer seven miles east of Gresford.

There are interesting similarities between werewolves, Black Dogs and Alien Big Cats

(ABCs). A Black Dog (gwyllgi) was encountered near Ruthin and recorded by T Gwynn Jones in *Welsh Folklore and Custom*: 'My grandmother declared that as she and my grandfather were riding on horseback from Ruthin one evening, in passing a roadside house, the nag suddenly shied and pressed to the hedge. At the moment a very tall mastiff was passing on the other side. My grandfather who rode behind saw nothing and his horse had not been startled. They had just come to live in the district and only got to know afterwards that the house had the reputation of being haunted.'

Further south, one Mr Edward Jones was returning late at night from a fair at Cynwyd, near Corwen. A terrifying spectral Black Dog chased him across the moor. He said it was 'a beast of fearsome visage and blood-shot eye'.

ABCs are said by some to be the modern version of the Black Dog. Having spent some time in South Africa and Kenya, I'm familiar with the elusive nature of big cats such as leopards, but in Britain ABCs seem to be ultra-elusive, almost supernatural in their nature.

Walk 10

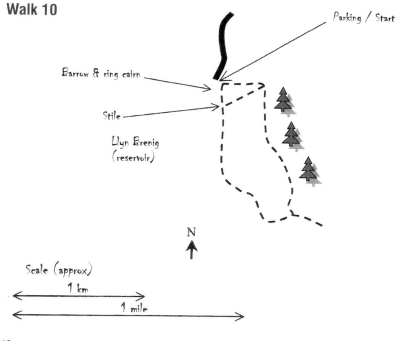

Parking / Start

Barrow & ring cairn

Stile

Llyn Brenig
(reservoir)

N

Scale (approx)
1 km
1 mile

Bronze Age platform cairn at Llyn Brenig

They are often described as 'black' and 'the size of a large dog' and are frequently seen at locations that were traditionally the preserve of Black Dogs. Perhaps in some cases they are one and the same. Where we once saw fairies, we now see aliens. The ABC could be the 'updated' Black Dog. A number of ABCs have been seen in the vicinity of the Denbigh Moors. Could werewolves, Black Dogs and their Alien Big Cat 'cousins' still stalk these lonely uplands?

Walk 10 – Llyn Brenig (Archaeological Trail)

WALK INFORMATION:
START/ PARKING: North-east side of Llyn Brenig signposted from the B4501 (road to Denbigh) GR SH983574
RECOMMENDED MAP: OS Explorer 264 or Landranger 116
DISTANCE (APPROX): 3.2km / 2 miles
TIME (APPROX): 1 to 2 hours (depending on how much time is spent at interpretation points)
WALK TYPE: Circular
DIFFICULTY RATING: Easy
NOTES: There are a number of interesting trails to follow in the vicinity of the reservoir – for more details visit the Llyn Brenig Visitor Centre.

I spent many days wandering the vast landscapes of the Hiraethog, and one day came across something quite unique. The Llyn Brenig Archaeological Trail captures the spirit of the Denbigh Moors and provides an excellent introduction to the diversity of landscapes and archaeology to be found in the area. The Bronze Age archaeology is particularly breathtaking. If ghosts haunt certain ancient archaeological remains, this trail is surely haunted.

The trail is so well waymarked and interpreted, it requires little in the way of a description. When you reach the car park you will see an interpretation board with a full route map. You can purchase the full 'Man at Brenig' leaflet at Llyn Brenig Visitor Centre.

The trail can be undertaken as a 'long' route or a 'short' route or both. Since the long route is only about 2 miles (3.2km) I would suggest this is the best option.

Walk 11

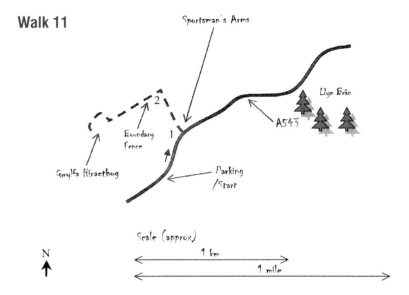

Sportsman's Arms

Llyn Brân

A543

2

Boundary Fence

1

Gwylfa Hiraethog

Parking /Start

Scale (approx)

1 km

1 mile

N

If you decide to walk the trail without a leaflet, I would suggest walking down the road to view Broncyn Arian Round Barrow and the nearby ring cairn, turning left over a nearby stile, walking up towards the conifer plantation and following the trail in a clockwise direction. Look out for waymarker posts and interpretation points along the way. The trail crosses enclosed farmland so it is very important to observe the Countryside Code.

Walk 11 – Gwylfa Hiraethog

WALK INFORMATION:
PARKING/START: Lay-by opposite Sportsman's Arms GR SH951587
RECOMMENDED MAP: OS Explorer 264 or Landranger 116
DISTANCE (APPROX): 2km / 1.2 miles
TIME (APPROX): 45 minutes to 1 hour
WALK TYPE: Linear
DIFFICULTY RATING: Easy
NOTES: At the time of writing a stile was missing at the fence just before the open moorland.

1. Follow a waymarker to the left of the pub and cross a stile. Walk past a broken stile to the field corner. Clamber over blocks to go through a gate leading onto the open moor.

2. Turn left and follow the fence line to reach Gwylfa Hiraethog. Note that the site is potentially dangerous, and is best viewed from the perimeter fence.

Nannau Nasties

The great estate of Nannau can be found a little north of Dolgellau, within sight of Cadair Idris. This noble seat dates back to AD 1100 and was founded by Cadwgan, a one-time prince of Powys. The mansion itself lies at 700 feet (200m) and is said to be the highest of its kind in Britain.

Above the estate can be found the 405m (1329ft) hill known as Foel Offrwm. This hill has a sinister reputation as a site of human sacrifice during the druidic 'dark ages' of Wales. In those times, victims were thrown from the cliff that overlooks Nannau, as a sacrifice to the pagan gods of old.

A little to the west lies a lake with an evil reputation. Llyn Cynwch is a gateway to the Underworld or fairy realm (a man once fell into

Foel Offrwm, hill of human sacrifice, as seen from the Precipice Walk

Llyn Cynwch is the home of a hungry demon that demands at least one human sacrifice every year

the lake and found himself in a land of great beauty). A monstrous water dragon (afanc) from Llyn Cynwch was killed by a local shepherd and buried on the hill above the lake. The burial site was once known as Carnedd Bedd y Wiber (The Dragon's Grave).

Sometimes a demonic entity emerges from the lake, crying 'the hour is come but not the man'. Anyone hearing this will be dragged into the lake. Some say that the demon requires at least once sacrifice per year – if its appetite isn't satisfied you could hear the aforementioned call and be the next victim.

Lying between the 'hill of sacrifice' and Llyn Cynwch, the Nannau Estate is naturally haunted to an unusual degree. One famous story concerns the Ceubren yr Ellyl or the 'Hollow Tree of the Demon/Goblin'.

It is said that Hywel Sele, Lord of Nannau and cousin of Owain Glyndŵr, was a supporter of Henry VI. In 1402 Glyndŵr visited his cousin at Nannau to try to win his support. It seems that Sele's loyalty to the king was absolute, as he took a walk with Glyndŵr in the deer park and was never seen again.

Forty years later Sele's skeleton was discovered in the hollow trunk of an old oak that had been struck by lightning. The haunted tree had been much feared by locals – to the extent that they avoided walking past it at night. Although the

tree toppled to the ground in 1813, some say it occasionally reappears.

The crossroads where the Dolgellau to Llanfachreth road crosses the road from the deer park to the mansion is haunted ground. A woman was seduced by one of the lords of Nannau and he murdered her when she became demanding (along with her pet dog). Once, her ghost was seen in the middle of the night in a long dress, little dog in tow, near the crossroads. A curious witness followed her until she disappeared by a small stone bridge. The bridge was investigated, based on the sighting, and the skeleton of a woman and a small dog were discovered.

Near the crossroads lies Ffynnon y Mulod (the Mule's Well). A groom once took his horse to be watered here and the animal was disturbed by a sudden gust of wind. The animal shied violently and trampled the groom to death. His screams and moans can be heard at night along with the wild snorts and whinnying of the stallion.

Walk 12 – The Precipice Walk

WALK INFORMATION:
START/ PARKING: GR SH754211 (follow the signs from Dolgellau)
RECOMMENDED MAP: OS Explorer OL18 or Landranger 124
DISTANCE (APPROX): 5km / 3 miles

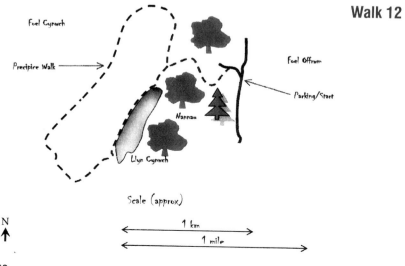

Walk 12

Foel Cynwch

Precipice Walk

Foel Offrwm

Parking/Start

Nannau

Llyn Cynwch

Scale (approx)

1 km

1 mile

N

The Nannau Estate: steeped in legend and haunted by a number of ghosts

TIME (APPROX): 1.5 hours
WALK TYPE: Circular
DIFFICULTY RATING: Moderate
NOTES: There are particularly fine views of Cadair Idris from this walk.

The 'Precipice Walk' is so well waymarked (and very easy to follow) that it needs little in the way of a route description. As well as sinister spots along the trail itself, this is a fantastically easy way to view Cadair Idris, Wales's 'most supernatural mountain', and the Mawddach Estuary.

To get started on the walk, turn left out of the car park and follow the road for a short distance to turn left along a signposted track. Follow the waymarkers past a farmhouse and cross two stiles to the start of the circular route, not far from the lake on your left. The walk can be undertaken in either direction, but anticlockwise is recommended.

The Haunted Goblin Stone Moor

The Carrey y Bwci (Goblin Stone) can be found alongside the ancient Roman road of Sarn Helen on a lonely moorland ridge near Lampeter, Ceredigion. The site consists of a mound with a large hollow in the centre (or a circular bank). In the middle lies the enormous haunted stone. Archaeologically, the site is something of an enigma. Theories as to the original function of the site include a round barrow, chambered tomb or even a Roman watchtower.

Locals are said to fear this spot. In *Places of Power*, Paul Devereux relates an interesting piece of folklore. In the 1940s a farmer approached the stone with the intension of breaking it up for gateposts. A violent thunderstorm ensued which followed the terrified farmer home. It is also said that three men were killed by lightning whilst standing next to the stone.

A lady who has now moved to Canada used to live in the area and hints at strange goings-on at the stone on her personal website. These include bolting horses, strange ceremonies and unusual mists. She was warned by local villagers not to go near the stone in the summer months – presumably because of the danger of being struck by lightning, or perhaps because of something more sinister.

A number of 'goblin stones' were known throughout Wales. The Carreg y Bwci is sometimes confused with similarly sinister stones, including the Goblin Stone of Cynwyl Gaio, near Llandovery.

It seems few people would pass this particular stone at night. In the seventeenth century a

A 'place of power': the haunted Goblin Stone in its moorland setting

Locals are said to be wary of the stone, in particular because it seems to act as some sort of 'lightning conductor'

Walk 13

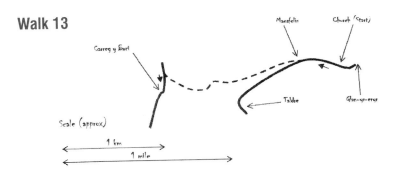

Carreg y Bwci
Maesfelin
Church (Start)
Taldre
Glan-yr-eryr

Scale (approx)

1 km

1 mile

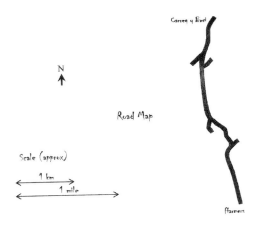

N

Carreg y Bwci

Road Map

Scale (approx)

1 km

1 mile

Ffarmers

'Boys, keep off the moors. Stay on the road.' If you've seen the film
An American Werewolf in London, *this junction will look somewhat familiar*

young man in search of work made the mistake of sleeping next to the stone. At midnight he was awoken by someone pinching his arms and ears and pricking his nose. By the light of the stars he saw the form of a goblin sitting on the stone with a number of others around him. Although the young man tried to make his escape, the chief goblin ordered his minions to restrain him. They tortured him until first light, when the goblins vanished. When the unfortunate jobseeker related his story to some passers-by he was informed he had slept under the cursed goblin stone.

In *Haunted Wales*, Richard Holland relates the story of the Cadair y Bwgan (Goblin Chair), located in a roadside verge a few miles from Brynteg, along the road to Maenaddwyn, Anglesey. The bwgan was a malevolent phantom who used to terrorise the neighbourhood before retiring back to his 'chair'.

Walk 13 – Carreg y Bwci

WALK INFORMATION:
START/PARKING: Near a small church at GR SN662481 (about 3km/1.5 miles north-east of Ffarmers)
RECOMMENDED MAP: OS Explorer OL17 or Landranger 115
DISTANCE (APPROX): 3.2km / 2 miles
TIME (APPROX): 1.5 hours
WALK TYPE: Linear
DIFFICULTY RATING: Moderate
NOTES: You can drive to the Carreg y Bwci at GR SN645479. From Ffarmers, head towards Llandewi Brefi, and take the turnings shown on the map.

With your back to the church, turn right and follow the road, crossing a bridge to reach a white stone cottage on the right (Maesfelin). Follow the track to the right of the building and go through the gate. Follow the fairly steep track up the hill until you reach a road. Turn left along the road – the Carreg y Bwci is just after the cattle grid on the right-hand side. To return, reverse the route.

An American Werewolf in Wales

Picture the scene. Two Americans get dropped off by a farmer at a junction on a lonely single-track road. As night approaches, they seek shelter and food at a tiny village pub called 'The Slaughtered Lamb'. Ignoring advice to 'beware the moon' and 'stick to the road' they stray off track and get lost on the moor. It is a full moon. In the mist and darkness, they hear the sound of a monster.

Although the cult film *An American Werewolf in London* was supposed to be set on the Yorkshire moors, the actual locations were Hay Bluff and the nearby village of Crickadarn, just off the A470 between Brecon and Builth Wells. The location managers couldn't have picked a more enigmatic area.

The remains of a Bronze Age stone circle can be seen very near to the spot where the stars of the film were dropped off by the farmer at the start of the film, and the road itself is steeped in history. The Gospel Pass acquired its name after the Third Crusade passed here, preaching and fundraising, in the twelfth century.

Close by in Hay on Wye stands the real Baskerville Hall (said to be haunted by a number of ghosts). The Baskervilles were related to the Dukes of Normandy and came to Britain to help William the Conquerer in 1066. Thomas Mynors Baskerville built the hall in 1839.

Sir Arthur Conan Doyle was a family friend, and it is said that on one of his numerous visits he heard local legends about spectral hounds. Perhaps the surrounding moors further inspired the writing of *The Hound of the Baskervilles*. It is said that Conan Doyle used Dartmoor as a fictional setting to deter tourists from harassing his Baskerville friends.

As Hay Bluff is a known haunt of the Hag of the Mist (see next walk) you are more likely to be led off your chosen path by her than by a werewolf. However, Alien Big Cats are regularly seen in the surrounding areas – perhaps the 'updated' werewolf or Black Dog.

Whatever happens, a walk here on a full-moon night could be quite an 'interesting' experience, particularly if you watch a certain film or read a certain book, just before you go.

Crickadarn village. The cottage to the left of the church doubled as 'The Slaughtered Lamb' pub. Even if you haven't seen the film, you will probably be aware of the scene where two strangers walk into a noisy pub and the pub falls silent

Atmospheric: the moors around Hay Bluff. Baskerville Hall (now the Baskerville Hall Hotel) can be found in nearby Hay on Wye. Sir Arthur Conan Doyle was a Baskerville family friend and he is thought to have based the story of the Hound of the Baskervilles on local legends

Walk 14

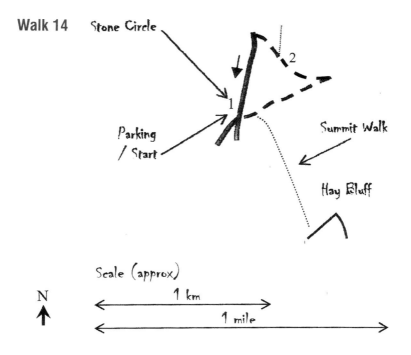

Walk 14 – Hay Bluff

WALK INFORMATION:
START/ PARKING: Car park adjacent to Bronze Age stone circle GR SO239373
RECOMMENDED MAP: OS Explorer OL13 or Landranger 161
DISTANCE (APPROX): 1.6km / 1 mile
TIME (APPROX): 30 minutes (allow one hour for summit walk)
WALK TYPE: Circular or linear
DIFFICULTY RATING: Easy (short walk); Moderate (summit walk)
NOTES: The summit walk is very steep. Combine with a trip to nearby Llanthony and Wiral Wood (See *Haunted Woods and Wooded Lanes*).

1. With your back to the car park, turn right up the road. Just before the junction (the drop-off point in the film) and a road sign on the left, turn left along a partially defined grassy track, heading towards the 'point' of Hay Bluff. After about 15m (15 yards), bear left (unless you feel like attempting the extremely steep scramble straight on to the summit). Ford a stream at an eroded section of the track, and then about 50m (50 yards) from the stream hollow you will reach another track. This is the Offa's Dyke Path. It is fairly easy to spot as the well-defined line of the path can be seen to your right. Turn left along the dyke path to reach a stone waymarker that reads 'CRASWALL'.

2. Ford the stream (the same one you crossed a few minutes ago), and continue along the well-defined track for about 50m (50 yards) to where the track splits in two. The split is easy to miss. The right fork continues downhill, whereas the left-hand path (Offa's Dyke Path) is reasonably level and continues towards a patch of gorse. Take the left fork and follow the path to reach a waymarker post next to the road. Turn left to follow the road uphill to the car park.

The Hag of the Moors

Although Hay Bluff (see Walk 14 above) is an occasional haunt of the Hag of the Mist, she is more frequently seen and sensed on a mountain ridge between Blaenavon and Abertillery in South Wales. This bleak ridge dominates the post-industrial landscapes of Torfaen and Blaenau Gwent below (part of the ridge is within a UNESCO World Heritage Site). A myriad of names subdivide the mountain – Mynydd Varteg Fawr, Mynydd Coety (Coity Mountain), Milfraen Mountain (sometimes used interchangeably with Coity Mountain) and many others. Look at an OS map, however, and you will see that this is a geographically distinct area of high moorland. For practical purposes we can consider it to be one mountain, an ancient geographical boundary that separates unitary authorities to this very day.

At first, these moors don't seem like a likely setting for fairies, wizardry, witchcraft and ghosts, but they certainly are; and supernatural phenomena have been reported quite recently.

Once, there was a strong belief in the existence of fairies in this area. Indeed, as recently as 1936 there were reports of the miraculous appearance of a fairy circle on the mountain. Storms and high winds were once attributed to two practitioners of black magic said to have lived on opposite sides of the ridge.

The ridge itself once provided a useful route south. A lonely old medieval mountain road traversed the ridge, and it is on this road – now just an eroded track – at an isolated spot near the once famous Cold Springs (Ffynhonnau Oerion), that most supernatural experiences are reported.

The waters of the springs were once thought to have healing powers, and hunters would stop at this point to slake their thirst. Once, a witch called Old Anne foresaw the location of some lost mules belonging to a man by the name of Robert ap Watkin – a mule driver. The mules were his livelihood, and each night he turned them out on the mountain to forage. He had refused to lend one to Old Anne, and suspected she had a hand in their disappearance. Even though he had searched the spot previously, she later told him where to find his mules (all eleven of them) – at the Cold Springs. When he searched the spot again, the mules were there.

The ridge to the northwest of the springs (Cefn Coch) is haunted by 'Scotch Cattle.' This was the name given to early trade unionists who blackened their faces and went disguised in animal skins.

In *A Relation of Apparitions of Spirits in the County of Monmouth and the Principality of Wales* Reverend Edmund Jones related some interesting tales about the moors. The most feared

The 'Old Woman of the Mountains' or 'Hag of the Mist' haunts this lonely ridge above Blaenavon. She was seen and heard as recently as 1994.

supernatural entity was the mysterious 'Hag of the Mountains' or Gwrach y Rhybin (Hag of the Warning) sometimes referred to as the 'Hag of the Mist.'

Locally, she was thought to have been a witch called Juan White, said to have lived 'time out of mind' somewhere nearby, but she may be much older. The Gwrach y Rhybin is a form of Welsh banshee, and she echoes in many ways the Celtic mother goddess Anu or Danu. Wirt Sikes identifies her with the Gwyllion – 'female fairies of frightful characteristics,who haunt lonely roads in the Welsh mountains, and lead night wanderers astray.'

The Gwyllion resemble the ancient Greek goddess Hecate, whose name means 'the distant one' or 'the remote one' – a guardian of roads and remote places. She is often accompanied by the Hounds of Hell.

A number of reports refer to travellers becoming hopelessly lost on this ridge, even when they know the mountain well. According to the 'Old Prophet' Jones, 'I once met a woman of the next Parish, who, together with her young daughter, had lost her way in the day-time, and was very weary, especially the young lass, whom I put in the way. I lost the way myself two or three times, in the day-time, on this Mountain, though I knew it very well, and that it is no more than a mile and a half long, and about half-a-mile broad.' Furthermore, 'another time, on going over the Mountain on horseback, on a misty day, and thinking she [the hag] might be near me, (for she was very busy on that Mountain observing who passed over it) I said in faith, "Do thy worst thou Old Devil, I will not lose my way"; and I did not at that time.'

John ap John of Coome Celin (Cwm Celin) had the following experience near the Cold Springs whilst en-route to Caerleon fair. John was travelling very early in the morning, before dawn, when suddenly, 'on going up hill on Milvre [Milfrean / Coity] Mountain, he heard a shouting behind him as if it were on Bryn Mawr, — which is a part of the black mountain in Breconshire, and soon after heard the shouting at Bwlch y Llwyn on his left hand, nearer to him; upon which, he became oppressed with fear, and heavy in walking; and began to suspect it was no human but a diabolical voice, designed to frighten him; having wondered before what people could be shouting on the mountain so early in the morning. Being come up to the higher part of the mountain, he heard the shouting at Gilvach fields on the right — before him, which confirmed his fear: but, being past the

The site of Ffynhonnau Oerion (the Cold Springs) is still clearly shown on modern maps

Gilvach fields, in the way to the cold springs, he heard something coming behind him like the noise of a coach; and what increased his fear the more, was the voice of a woman with the coach which he heard crying WOW UP. Now, as he knew that no coach could go that way, and hearing the noise of a coach approaching nearer and nearer, he was certain it must be an evil Spirit following him; he was very much terrified; and fearing he should see some horrid appearance, he walked a short distance from the path and lay down with his face towards the heath, fearing to look about until it had passed him: when it was gone out of hearing — he arose; and hearing the birds singing as the day began to break, also seeing some sheep before him, his fear went quite off.'

Supernatural experiences in the Cold Springs area continue to this day. A number of witnesses have reported strange hooded figures on the mountain, and the Hag of the Moors was seen as recently as 1994. She was preceded by the sound of invisible galloping horses.

Walk 15 – Coity Mountain

WALK INFORMATION:
START/PARKING: Garn Lakes upper car park GR SO230103
RECOMMENDED MAP: OS Explorer OL13 or Landranger 161
DISTANCE (APPROX): 5km / 3 miles
TIME (APPROX): 1.5 to 2 hours
WALK TYPE: Part circular
DIFFICULTY RATING: Moderate
NOTES: Don't cross the off-path section of open moor in poor visibility.

Walk 15

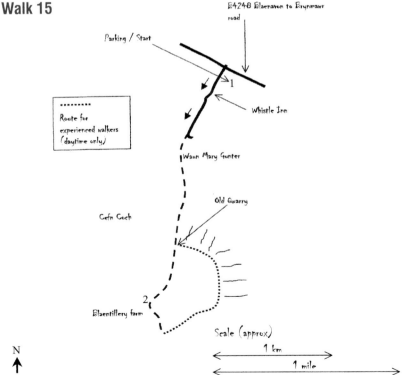

1. From the car park, turn left and follow the road, crossing a bridge before you pass the Whistle Inn on your left. Continue on along the track and cross a stile next to a field gate to reach a fingerpost directing you across a field. Cross the field to reach another gate and stile. Cross the stile and follow the track uphill, crossing a metalled mine road along the way (watch out for traffic). The path continues to ascend the hill, passing some railings near an old quarry near the top of the ridge. Soon, the path levels out and you will emerge onto the haunted moor. Continue on across the ridge, ignoring any paths leading left or right. Pass through a double fence marking the line of a gas pipeline (present at the time of writing but there are plans for its removal), to reach a drystone wall field boundary and gate.

2. Turn left at the walls and continue to the end. Continue along a path at the end of the walls until you reach a path bearing left uphill. If the light or weather is poor, I would suggest reversing your route at this point. If conditions are good and you are confident about your navigation skills, turn left and ascend the path. At the point where the path bends around to the right at the top of the ridge, turn left off the path to follow the line of the ridge back to the track above the quarry you passed earlier. Use the steep ground on your right as a 'handrail' over the open ground and remember to exercise caution as there are steep drops near the quarry. Due to the possibility of hidden 'ankle-breaking' fissures and holes in this area, you will need to tread very cautiously. In particular, avoid walking across the open ground in snow and poor light.

The All-Seeing Sentinel

'As soon as I saw anything I saw Twyn Barlwm, that mystic tumulus, the memorial of peoples that dwelt in that region before the Celts left the Land of Summer.'

(From Arthur Machen's *Far off Things*)

Can a landscape or a feature in a landscape possess some sort of awareness? Are mysterious supernatural phenomena merely a manifestation of a much greater landscape mystery?

The silhouette of Twm Barlwm (also known as Twyn Barlwm or Twmbarlwm) near Newport in south-east Wales is 'burned' into the collective consciousness of the local population. This 419m/1,375ft-high hill can be seen for miles around and is topped by a distinctive 'tump' or 'pimple'.

Historian J H Clark described Twm Barlwm as 'The Hill of the Judge', and the nearby Dyffryn y Gladdfa (Valley of the Graves) was where the condemned were executed or buried. The origins of the mound are unclear. Clark says, 'On the summit is a tumulus or artificial mound of earth and stones, surrounded by a deep fosse, supposed by some to have been a beacon, by others a place of sepulchre, or devoted to Bardic assemblies.' The tump lies at the eastern end of what is probably an Iron Age hill fort – though it may have had its origins in the Bronze Age. It has also been suggested that the hill was once used for sun worship.

A haunting is said to occur at a pool of water on the hill called The Pool of Avarice. Strange cries are said to emanate from the waters on stormy nights. This mysterious place is also a fairy haunt. The fairies on the hill are said to take the form of swarms of bees (an old tale tells of a battle between bees and wasps on the hill). In *British Goblins*, Wirt Sikes suggested that swarms of bees were thought to be fairies in disguise.

In *Mysterious Wales*, Chris Barber describes an odd event on Twm Barlwm relating to the bees and wasps of the hill. In 1984 a team of countryside workers attempted to repair damage to the tump caused by off-road bikes. As they were constructing some wooden steps they were 'buzzed' by a swarm of bees. On returning to their vehicle they found it covered by the swarm. Indeed, it would seem that the tump is protected by supernatural beings. In 1830 a band of navvies attempted to excavate the mound, but were thwarted by thunder and lightning.

The tump is particularly famous for its music – yes, music. It is said to float down the mountain slopes, and can enchant children in the style of the Pied Piper of Hamelin. One child is said to have followed the music and was never seen again. This young girl was said to have become obsessed with the hill. She was convinced that

The familiar profile of Twm Barlwm

it was a living being and knew everything about the local village (probably Risca) and its inhabitants. One day the she left the village and headed for the hill – never to be seen again. Some reports say she was 'lured' by the ghostly music of Twm Balwm. Hard evidence for the existence of the music was obtained when a local family managed to make a recording.

A friend of the author, who is a keen walker, has also heard the music. Caron told me that she was sitting on the tump at around 9pm one fine June evening. The sun was setting, and the scene was idyllic. Suddenly, a strange sound caught her ear. Caron said that it sounded like bagpipes. At first she wondered who could be playing them in such a remote spot. 'My initial reaction was that I felt slightly sorry for the lonely piper.' It soon became apparent that there was nobody there. Many others have heard the mysterious music, which is sometimes described as sounding like that of an organ. On the BBC's 'Weird Wales' website, 'Simon' describes a similar experience to that of Caron. He describes driving up the lane to the south of the hill, where you can park fairly close to the tump. At around 2am, he heard the sound of 'chains being dragged up the stone path', 'footsteps' which seemed to be

getting nearer and the sound of organ music. From his account, it seems he left the area in quite a hurry, vowing never to return. I believe the experience took place near OS grid reference ST248925 if you would like to hear the music for yourself.

It will come as no surprise that the hill is a favoured spot for UFOs. In September 1980 more than twenty factory workers in Rogerstone, near Newport, saw a landed UFO just to the right of the tump. It was variously described as 'a silver oval dome made of aluminium' and a 'massive, white, oblong just like a double-decker bus resting on the ground'.

Twm Barlwm is a very, very haunted place, worthy of further investigation. Don't forget your dictaphone!

Walk 16

To Visitor Centre / Cwmcarn

Parking / Start

To Forest Drive

2

Raven Walk

'Tump'

3

Scale (approx)

N

1 km

1 mile

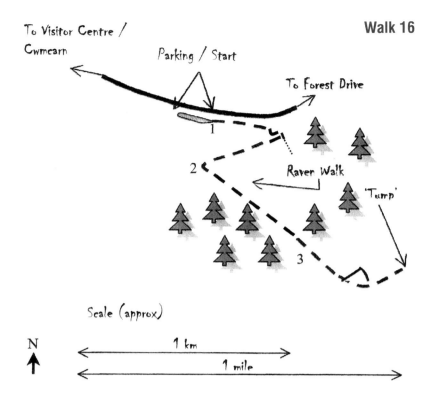

Walk 16 – Twm Barlwm

WALK INFORMATION:
START/PARKING: Lake above Cwmcarn Forest Drive Visitor Centre at GR ST233934
RECOMMENDED MAP: OS Explorer 152 or Landranger 171
DISTANCE (APPROX): 4km / 2.5 miles
TIME (APPROX): 1.5 to 2 hours
WALK TYPE: Linear
DIFFICULTY RATING: Energetic (steep ascents)
NOTES: There is an alternative access road to the south of the hill from Risca (GR ST248925).

1. From the narrow end of the lake, walk up a footpath via a wooden barrier. Cross a walkway over a pond, bear right and walk through a gap in a fence and up some steps. Follow the path uphill, climb some more steps and turn left to go through a gate. Descend for a short distance and turn right up a footpath where a fingerpost indicates 'Twm Barlwm 1.3km'. Go through the gate and continue up the track to a path junction and a waymarker post. Do not cross the stile ahead of you. Instead, turn right back in the direction of the lake, bearing left and uphill near cycleway post 3. Turn right along the road and continue straight along a track. Turn left just before a green vehicle barrier to double back uphill along the Raven Walk.

2. Follow the well-worn forest path up the steep hill, ascending two sets of steps to reach the road. Cross the road, pass a sculpture and head up to the kissing gate leading onto the open common.

3 Follow the path up the very steep hill in the direction of the 'Castle Mound'. Pass through old earthworks, pass the trig point and continue on to 'the tump' (accessed via some steps).

Mysterious organ music, UFOs and frightening experiences have been reported in the vicinity of the 'tump'

Further Exploration

More Weird Moors, Bogs and Hills

There seem to be an endless number of haunted moors, hills and wild boggy 'wastes' in Wales. Many of these areas have now been mapped as 'Access Land', which means you can wander freely.

The Witch's Pool

This pool on Flint Mountain in north-east Wales is known as Pwll-yr-Wrach or 'The Witch's Pool.' In 1852 a farm labourer was attacked by a man-shaped supernatural being from the lake, The full story can be read in Richard Holland's *Haunted Wales.*

The Borth Bog Ghost-Witch

According to *The Paranormal Database*, a seven-foot tall ghost witch is said to haunt Cors Fochno (Borth Bog) in Ceredigion, mid-Wales. She makes people ill by breathing on them.

Drum Demons

Mynydd y Drum is a hill south of Ystadgynlais in the southern part of Powys. A series of

Bronze Age cairns can be found in a line on the moorland top. One cairn in particular has an evil reputation. Just as the pyramids of Egypt have their supernatural guardians, the ancient burial cairn of Garn Goch (Red Cairn) has its own appointed protectors. Demons are said to guard a treasure within. Any attempt at inter-fering with the monument could be met with supernatural violence.

A wizard from Ystradgynlais found out about the treasure through supernatural means, but in order to get at it he needed an assistant to spend the night at the cairn whilst he set about his business. Eventually, he found a willing accomplice who agreed to take part in magical night-time ceremonies in return for half the treasure.

One cold, dark night they set about imple-menting their plan. They climbed up the hill to a grassy area directly adjacent to Garn Goch. The wizard needed to confront the demonic guardians of the treasure, so he got together his mystical apparatus, put on his ceremonial garments and traced two circles like a figure of eight in the grassy sward. He took out a great black grimoire (book of magic), lit a candle and stepped into one of the protective circles. He then instructed his assistant to step into the other circle and told him that under no circumstances should he step outside it.

The wizard opened the grimoire and repeated three times, 'I adjure and invocate thee by the silence of the night and by the holy rites of magic and by the number of the infernal legions, that without delay thou present thyself here and answer my demand by the force of the words contained in this book.'

The first entity to appear took the form of a monstrous bellowing bull. The assistant nervously held his ground and stayed within his circle. The bull disappeared. It was followed by a gigantic goat, which rushed at him before disappearing into thin air. These terrors were followed by a gigantic boar and a fire-breathing lion – but still he stood his ground. Worse was to follow. A huge roaring wheel of fire rushed at the assistant, and the shock caused him to step out of the ring. As soon as he did this a demon (or perhaps the Devil himself) grabbed him and uttered a curse to the effect that his life would last only as long as the wizard's candle. At this point the wizard blew out the candle and gave it to the unfortunate assistant.

He chastised him for stepping out of the circle but gave him some advice on preserving the candle: 'Put it in a cold place and your life will be safe.' This he did, but although it was never lit it didn't last very long. The assistant was never the same after the terrors he encountered that night. As his life was tied to the candle, the assistant's life ebbed away as the candle decayed. It was said that as soon as he died, his body went to the demons of Garn Goch.

The treasure was never discovered.

The Pool of Blood and Moaning?

A few miles south west of Crickhowell, South Wales, on the moors of Mynydd Llangatwg (Llangattock Mountain) can be found an extremely creepy pool of water called Pwll Gwyrhoc. The pool is known locally as 'Witches Pool', but a possible translation would be 'Pool of Blood and Moaning' (assuming gwy is a corruption of gwaed – the Welsh word for blood). The site was brought to my attention by Kevin Walker, a locally based hill walking and mountaineering instructor.

A great and bloody battle is said to have taken place here in the year 728 AD, between the British king Rhodri Molwynog, and Ethelbald, King of Mercia (though some say an even earlier battle took place between the Silures and the Ordivices – two of the five great Celtic tribes of Wales). The lake marks the centre of the battle, and became so trampled and poisoned with blood that the vegetation never grew back. As a result, the area gradually sank into the bog and became a lake. Stand on the shore and look near the horizon through 360 degrees and every high point has a burial cairn on it. In the 1960's a botanist camping on the moor witnessed 'hordes of tiny people' at a nearby bog, which he later found out was known as 'fairies bog.' Did the botanist really see fairies, or did the sighting represent a ghostly re-enactment of the aforementioned battle?

This is a very remote and lonely place. I'm told that it would be 'inadvisable' to spend the night here. Not somewhere to visit alone in the darkness, trust me. The lake is located at GR SO184153, in case you still want to visit.

A Haunted Pub and a Holy Hill

The ancient Skirrid Mountain Inn could make the ideal haunted accommodation from which to explore a haunted region and numerous locations in this book. The inn is named after the nearby Skirrid, a hill near Abergavenny that was once known as 'Holy Mountain'.

The connection between the mysterious hill and this seriously haunted pub is the reason for its inclusion in this book. The Skirrid is steeped in folklore and history. The most famous stories concern the great fissure in the hill, which was said to have opened up at the precise time of he crucifixion. Traces of an ancient chapel (St Michael's) can be found near the top.

The Skirrid Mountain Inn dates from 1110 and is haunted by numerous ghosts. These are said to include some of the 180 rebels from the Monmouth Rebellion who were hanged here in 1685. The hanging beam can still be viewed, complete with rope marks. Wales's 'Oldest Inn' was investigated by Living TV's *Most Haunted* team in 2003.

Tangible Strangeness

Once known locally as 'the moors', the Gwent Levels are the Welsh version of the more famous Somerset Levels, and comprise an area of low-lying land south of Newport. The man-made landscape is one of the largest surviving areas of ancient grazing marshes and reen (drainage ditch) systems in Britain. This is a landscape of acknowledged national importance. According to Glamorgan-Gwent Archaeological Trust the levels hold 'extraordinarily diverse environmental and archaeological potential'.

Many ghosts haunt this strange landscape. At night-time an extraordinary atmosphere prevails, unlike any place I have visited in Wales. Catherine Fisher captures this atmosphere in her book *The Candle Man*.

The Ring Cairn of Power

Carn Lechart can be found on the moors above Pontardawe in the Swansea Valley. This impressive Bronze Age ring cairn is said to harbour a mysterious invisible force. Two paranormal investigators were attacked by the force after standing inside the monument, and one was physically 'evicted' from the ring of stones. Later, the pair became ill and felt 'drained' of energy.

The Hill of Visions

Mynydd Carningli (Mountain of Angels) is a 400m/1,300ft-high hill near Newport, Pembrokeshire. The hill is all that remains of a 450 million-year-old volcano, and was used in the Iron Age as a hill fort. Numerous enclosures and hut circles can be seen – evidence that a large number of people once lived (and died) on the hill.

Some maintain that if the hill is viewed from the south, you can see the profile of the sleeping earth goddess – head, breast, stomach and raised knees. Many maintain the hill is (and always has been) sacred.

There is a tradition of conversing with the supernatural on Carningli that continues to this day. This tradition is said to have originated when the fifth-century St Brynach sought refuge on the hill and conversed with divine beings.

The 'sacred hill of visions' is known to produce strange magnetic anomalies. Compass needles behave erratically in proximity to the hill and strange bodily sensations have been reported. Odd lights are still seen to this day. In *The Spirit Paths of Wales*, Laurence Main claimed to have seen earth lights three nights in a row on Carningli in November 1996. Perhaps the lights were the same divine beings of old.

Haunted Woods and Wooded Lanes

'A tradition is current in Mathavarn, in the parish of Llanwrin, and the Centre of Cyfeillioc, concerning a certain wood called Ffridd yr Ywen (the Forest of the Yew,) that it is so called on account of a magical yew-tree which grows exactly in the middle of the forest. Under that tree there is a fairy circle called The Dancing Place of the Goblin.'

(From Wirt Sikes, *British Goblins*)

Once, there was a wildwood – a gnarled and primeval landscape that covered much of the British mainland. The wildwood was untouched by civilisation. Nature ran riot. Then came man – and within a relatively short time, the wildwood was in ruins. Today, one would need to visit Eastern Europe or North America to gain any measure of what the great wood was like all those thousands of years ago.

Although the wildwood of old is long gone, something of it seems to linger in our genes. There are very few people who wouldn't feel nervous if they found themselves alone in a dark wood. I suspect we are programmed to be wary of the woods at night – after all, in historical terms it wasn't that long ago that bears, wolves and other great beasts could be encountered in the darkness of the forest.

The native woods of historic times were haunted places to many rural folk, a link between 'civilisation' and primal nature, and a reminder of pre-Christian beliefs such as nature worship.

Today, the ancient woods of Wales are precious but fragmented echoes of the primeval forest, places where strange and inexplicable things might still happen. Everybody knows 'the haunted wood' of myth and fairy tale, but most would be hard pressed to locate a genuine example. Here are a few…

The Gloddaeth Woods Goblin

Gloddaeth Woods can be found a little south of Llandudno – 'where the mountains of Snowdonia meet the sea'. This ancient wood is the setting for a strange and disturbing story.

At one time people were paid to hunt and destroy foxes and other vermin that were numerous in the wood. One day a certain Thomas

Gloddaeth Woods lie between the sea and the mountains, and are the setting for a strange and disturbing story

Davies was looking for signs of foxes in the wood when he chanced upon a den. As an experienced countryman, he could tell from the burrow that there were cubs in the hole. Thomas immediately set about formulating a plan to eradicate the vixen and her young. Looking around he saw a large oak with forked branches – a perfect vantage point. He knew that come nightfall the vixen would leave the den to forage. At this time he would make his move and eradicate the creatures.

Night came, and from his tree-top hideout Thomas heard a blood-curdling scream from the direction of the sea. It sounded like a human in distress, but it seemed some way off so he decided to ignore it and focus on his quarry. The screams in the darkness came again, and they soon issued forth at regular intervals. Whatever was making the frightening sounds was coming closer.

Eventually the screams were very near and the understandably nervous Thomas saw what was approaching. There in front of him stood a terrifying creature. It was a nude, demonic-looking being, a hideous goblin with luminous eyes that burned like fire – eyes that were looking directly at him. It was only twelve yards away from him, and it crouched down, then stood up, crouched down, stood up – eyes fixed all the time on Thomas. He felt the being could spring at him at any moment, and feared his terror would cause him to lose his balance, at which point he would be at the mercy of the creature. He thought of firing his gun at the goblin, but couldn't summon the courage.

He closed his eyes, praying that when he opened them the creature would be gone. Every time he opened them, the glowing eyes were still there – staring with malevolent intent.

At 4am he heard a cock crow at Penrhyn Farm, and when he again opened his eyes, the creature had vanished.

The tale of the 'goblin' of Gloddaeth Woods is a haunted woodland 'classic.' Questions remain as to the creature's nature and intent. It would seem that the creature was an appointed 'guardian' of the woods. If seen today, it would no doubt be interpreted as extraterrestrial, especially since Gloddaeth Woods are but a stone's throw away from the Great Orme, Wales's most UFO-haunted location.

Walk 17 – Gloddaeth Woods

WALK INFORMATION:
START/PARKING: Near Llanrhos Church GR SH793803
RECOMMENDED MAP: OS Explorer OL17 or Landranger 115
DISTANCE (APPROX): 4km / 2.5 miles
TIME (APPROX): 1.5 hours
WALK TYPE: Circular
DIFFICULTY RATING: Moderate
NOTES: This walk involves crossing a very busy main road.

1. Facing the main road turn right up the path, passing a building to reach the old section of the cemetery and a footpath sign. Continue in the direction indicated by the sign to walk away from the main road and pass the cemetery on your right. Go through a metal kissing gate, through a small field (graveyard on your right), then go through another kissing gate. Zigzag down to the road and cross WITH EXTREME CAUTION. Zigzag up the bank to reach a kissing gate on the other side. Go through this, walk across the field and go through another kissing gate in the top right corner at the edge of the wood. Turn right along a track and go through a kissing gate between stone walls. Continue uphill and go through a metal kissing gate to follow a well-worn path and join a track near a building and bear left. Continue on to a ladder stile with Gloddaeth Hall (St David's College) on the right. Cross the stile and continue to a kissing gate.

2. Go through the gate and follow the path ahead up into the woods (ignore the path to the right leading to Gloddaeth Isaf). Continue up through the woods and go through a kissing gate. Follow the path and go through another kissing gate. Turn right to follow the wall with the woods to your right. Just before you drop down a slope near a building, turn diagonally left near an electricity pylon and follow a poorly defined path past some gorse to your right. In a short while, the path becomes more defined and roughly follows a short anticlockwise route around the building on your left (Hen Dwr – an old windmill). When you reach a road, turn right.

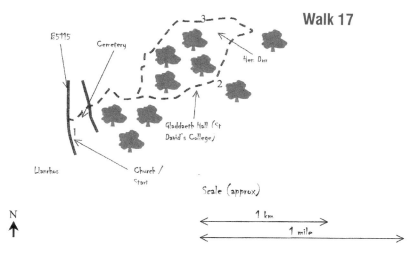

Walk 17

3. Walk down the road and just before the cattle grid and kissing gate turn left and immediately right down a driveway with a sign saying 'Private Drive Footpath Only'. Walk down to the end of this drive to follow a path leading up a bank on the left. Follow the footpath with a fence to the right and the woods to your left and pass through a gap between two fields. Continue in the direction indicted by waymarkers directing you downhill in a right–left zigzag below the cliffs on your left. Turn right just before a kissing gate with the stone wall now to your left, go through a kissing gate onto a track and where it bends around to the right go through a kissing gate next to a field gate on your left. Cross the field to go through the kissing gate leading down to road. Re-cross the road and go back through the kissing gate on the other side. Go through another kissing gate to reach the main road and return to the start point.

Gloddaeth Woods are home to a hideous goblin with luminous eyes that burn like fire

The Many Horrors of Wepre

Wepre Park can be found in Connah's Quay, north-east Wales. Within the park can be found some of the most haunted woods in all of Wales.

The park was once part of the Wepre Hall Estate. A visitor centre now stands on the site of Wepre Hall, which existed in various forms from at least the eleventh century to the 1960s when the last hall was demolished. It is probable that a Saxon dwelling existed on the site from as early as the seventh century.

The woods of Wepre Park were once a part of the great Forest of Ewloe, and in a corner of this forest Prince Llwelyn ap Gruffudd (known as Llewelyn the Last) finished building Ewloe Castle in about 1257.

This was a native Welsh castle, built only eight miles from the English stronghold of Chester – a relatively short-lived statement that said newly reconquered northern Flintshire belonged to the Welsh. Numerous battles and skirmishes between the English and the Welsh must have taken place in this disputed area.

The romantic castle ruins certainly add to the diversity of the woods, which hold a variety of attractions for the historian, geologist and naturalist alike. The woods will also be of special interest to another group: ghost hunters.

You may have heard of Sites of Special Scientific Interest (SSSIs), which are usually sites of great natural and/or geological importance. Sometimes I wonder if our haunted places should have some sort of special protection. Wepre would surely be one of the first of a new type of SSSI – the 'Site of Special *Supernatural* Interest!'

The 'horrors of Wepre' are best summarised as a list. They include:

• Ghostly pack of dogs – seen by multiple witnesses, sometimes associated with the pet cemetery near the visitor centre. Some of the reports could be classified as Gwyllgi sightings.

• Numerous frightening ghosts, including 'Nora the Nun' – the prolific, angry ghost of a faceless floating nun said to haunt the Rosie Pool, castle grounds, the waterfall near the old gardens and the lane between Wepre Inn and Northop Hall. There are various theories as to what happened to 'Nora'. These include her having had her head cut off after an affair with a monk; being hit by a World War II bomb

The ancient woods of Wepre Park were once a part of the great forest of Ewloe. More recently, they formed part of the Wepre Hall Estate. It is probable that a building existed at the site of Wepre Hall as early as the seventh century AD.

near the waterfall; or perhaps drowning herself in the Rosie Pool.

• The sound of drumming and marching feet in the vicinity of the castle.

• Mysterious lights seen in and around the castle.

• A headless horseman or the sound of galloping horses

• A luminous singing lady haunts the 'Welsh Tower' (the U-shaped keep) of the castle. She prefers to sing in stormy weather. She is also known to wander the ramparts and has been witnessed fairly recently. A castle custodian had a terrifying encounter with this ghost.

Walk 18 – Wepre Park and Ewloe Castle

WALK INFORMATION:
START/PARKING: Car park south of Wepre Drive, Connah's Quay (signposted Wepre Park) GR SJ295684
RECOMMENDED MAP: OS Explorer 266 or Landranger 117
DISTANCE (APPROX): 3.2km / 2 miles
TIME (APPROX): 1 to 1.5 hours
WALK TYPE: Circular
DIFFICULTY RATING: Easy

NOTES: For quick access to the castle area, park in the lay-by on the B5125 between Northop Hall and Ewloe, near a 'Ewloe Castle' sign (GR SJ286672). I would recommend combining a visit to Wepre Park with a visit to nearby Old Warren (see the next story).

1. At the information board (top left side of the car park near the play park), follow the path downhill with the play park to your right. The path converges with another at the bottom. Follow the path around to the right, passing the waterfalls and a bridge on the left to reach the boardwalk. Continue along the boardwalk to eventually reach a set of steps. At the top of the steps, turn left and follow a broad track with a stream valley to the left. Continue along the track, passing a track to the right and a sign on the left saying 'Castell Ewloe 15 Mins Walk'. Continue straight on, passing geological formations on the right. The path swings right then left and eventually descends some steps with railings on the left. Continue to a stone bridge on the left, cross and turn right at a junction in the path.

2. Continue to some steps on your right, descend the steps and cross a footbridge. Walk up the

Ewloe – a haunted castle in a haunted wood

Walk 18

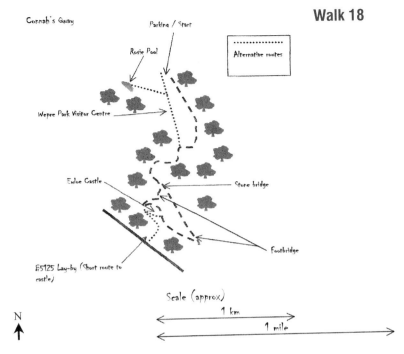

Connah's Quay

Parking / Start

Rosie Pool

Alternative routes

Wepre Park Visitor Centre

Ewloe Castle

Stone bridge

Footbridge

B5125 Lay-by (Short route to castle)

Scale (approx)

1 km

1 mile

N

---

track and ascend more steps. Follow the path as it bears right to reach a junction and some stone steps on the right. Descend the steps to walk around the castle in an anticlockwise direction. Halfway round you will reach some steps on your left. These allow access to the castle remains. Spend some time exploring the castle and return to the perimeter path. From the bottom of the steps leading up into the castle, continue around in an anticlockwise direction to reach some steps leading right down to a footbridge.

3. Cross the footbridge, pass a path on your left leading to 'Devil's Basin', and continue straight on passing the stone bridge you crossed earlier to your right. With the stream now on your right, you will ascend the steps, pass the geological formations on your left and re-pass the 'Castell Ewloe 15 Mins Walk' sign. Continue on to the steps on the right that lead back down to the boardwalk. At this point, you can either descend the steps to continue back the same way you came or continue straight on to pass the visitor centre and reach the car park.

The Floating Clergyman

In *Haunted Wales* Richard Holland tells the story of the frightening ghost of Old Warren in Broughton, Flintshire. The Old Warren is now an overgrown (and slightly sinister) dead-end road due to the construction of a bypass. It now leads walkers past the spooky Bilberry Wood, within which lies the 'suicide lake', as it is known locally. The area would make an excellent location for 'ghost walks' and outdoor paranormal investigations.

Old Warren is haunted by a floating elderly black-caped figure with an old clergyman's hat on his head. The ghost has an aversion to courting couples and is often seen to have an angry disapproving look on its face. On one occasion the ghost caused a victim's motorbike to suffer electrical disturbances in the form of a flickering headlamp after gliding past.

The identity of this frightening ghost is a mystery, but for now the assumption must be that it has something to do with the conspicuous old chapel at the beginning of the road. I suspect

Walk 19

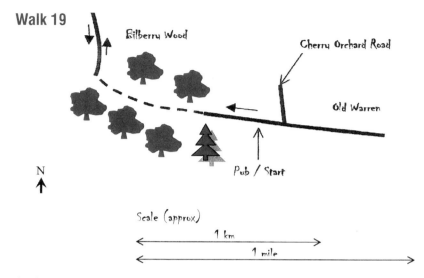

the ghost was a particularly stern character in life. Perhaps he still works to keep Old Warren 'respectable', even from beyond the grave.

Many local people have weird stories to tell about this heavily wooded area.

Cherry Orchard Road is said to be particularly 'active' in terms of ghostly phenomena.

Believe me when I say that as darkness falls, Old Warren and Bilberry Wood take on a certain sinister aspect. You'll see what I mean when you take an evening stroll.

Walk 19 –
Old Warren (short walk)

WALK INFORMATION:
START/PARKING: Near Spinning Wheel Public House GR SJ319635
RECOMMENDED MAP: OS Explorer 264 or Landranger 116
DISTANCE (APPROX): 2.5km / 1.5 miles
TIME (APPROX): 45 minutes
WALK TYPE: Linear
DIFFICULTY RATING: Easy
NOTES: There's plenty of roadside parking. If you prefer you can drive down to the locked gate marking the point where the road ends and park here instead of near the pub.

This very short linear walk starts at the Spinning Wheel public house on Old Warren. From the pub, turn left facing the road and continue to the end. Walk around the locked gate and walk down the old road with woods either side. At the end of the road the path narrows near the bypass on the left. Pass by a footbridge over the bypass to reach a wooden barrier to the left of a gate. At this point I would suggest you reverse the route to relive the terrors of Old Warren.

Walk 20
Old Warren- (long walk)

WALK INFORMATION:
START/PARKING: Tinkersdale public car park, Hawarden. GR SJ316657
RECOMMENDED MAP: OS Explorer 264 or Landranger 116
DISTANCE (APPROX): 8km / 5 miles
TIME (APPROX): 2 to 2.5 hours
WALK TYPE: Linear
DIFFICULTY RATING: Easy
NOTES: If you prefer, you can turn this walk into a circular route. Information on the route can be found in the car park. A full route description can be downloaded from Flintshire council's website (www.flintshire.gov.uk) – look for 'Enjoying our Countryside' under 'Leisure & Tourism'

Bilberry Wood lies adjacent to Old Warren and has an extremely spooky feel after dark

Old Warren is a 'road to nowhere' and is haunted by a floating black-caped figure with an old clergyman's hat on its head

This little chapel marks the start of Old Warren. Could there be a connection between the chapel and the haunting?

1. Find a waymarker at the back of the car park and turn right down a slope with rails. Follow a well-defined path through the wood past an eighteenth-century corn mill. The path bears right and crosses a bridge to eventually reach a gate and two stiles. Cross one of the stiles and continue straight on with walls to the left. Pass a broken stile and continue with walls to your left and the wood to the right. Cross another stile and follow the path past some old estate gates, ignoring tracks leading off to the right At a staggered path junction turn left then right, cross a brook and cross a stile. I believe one of the paths to the right, just before you leave the wood leads to the haunted 'suicide lake', as it is known locally (the lake is in a private woodland).

2. Leave the wood to continue along the road (Cherry Orchard Road). Cross a stile next to a cattle grid to reach Old Warren. Continue to the end as per the short walk and reverse the route.

The Wiral Witch Project

Wiral Wood lies above the ruins of the twelfth-century Llanthony Priory in the beautiful and wild Vale of Ewyas, deep within the Black Mountains of South Wales. The origins of the priory are said to be traceable to the sixth-century Dewi Sant: St David, patron saint of Wales.

St David was said to have erected a small chapel or cell on the site, which he used for prayer and meditation. The cell fell into ruins, and many hundreds of years later a Norman knight by the name of William de Lacy stumbled upon the cell whilst out hunting (some say he sought shelter during a violent storm). Whilst at the cell, de Lacy became a convert. He decided to live the life of a religious hermit and was soon joined by others who fell under the spell of the place. In 1108 a small church was built and dedicated to St David. Thus were the humble beginnings of the once great priory.

So remote was Llanthony that its isolation made it extremely vulnerable to attack. The location is a testament to the commitment of the people who worshiped here. Today, the isolated ruins attract visitors wanting to experience the wild and beautiful scenery, and perhaps experience the spiritual atmosphere that has deeply affected so many throughout the ages.

Walk 20

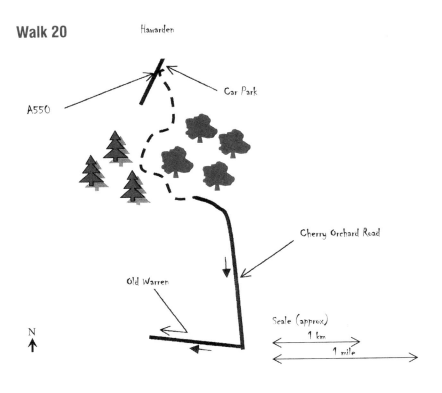

Hawarden

Car Park

A550

Cherry Orchard Road

Old Warren

Scale (approx)

1 km

1 mile

N

Spookscapes: a haunted priory, a haunted wood and a haunted mountain...

Wiral Wood, dominion of a shape-shifting witch

It would seem that the attachment to this area persists beyond the grave in some cases. Ghostly monks haunt the ruins, and the mountain above the priory has its fair share of spooks and spectres. A man travelling from Llanthony to Longtown crossed the mountain and became lost in fog. A figure wearing a large broad-brimmed hat and cloak put him back on the path. The ghost did not speak, but simply led the man to safety and disappeared. When visiting friends in Llanthony at a later date the man described his ghostly encounter, and was told it was a man who had been dead two years. Apparently, the dead man 'knew the mountain well'.

A local witch was supposed to have the power of turning into a crow and frequented the area. The old woman was a local fortune-teller and always wore a black shawl. She gained a reputation as someone who would supernaturally punish those that crossed her. It seems her favoured dominion was above the priory ruins in Wiral Wood.

Once, a group of children were playing in the wood and saw the witch. They began to taunt her and she turned into a crow and began to attack the children. The children ran toward the shelter of the priory for protection and looked back, only to see the figure of the old woman where the crow had been.

A shepherd once crossed the old woman to his cost. One day he came upon the old woman in his path whilst driving his sheep down a nearby mountain. The shepherd chastised her for being in his way, to which she responded with a cold stare, but no words. From then on, every time he drove his flock through the wood he and his sheep were harassed by a huge crow until they crossed a stream to the north of the wood (a boundary which the evil could not cross).

One moonlit night the rector of Llanthony saw the old witch standing in his churchyard surrounded by a group of figures. Moonlight shone straight through the bodies of the people, and he saw that she was conversing with the dead. In response to this he crossed himself, put a lighted candle in the window and tied a red ribbon around his baby daughter's cradle as protection from evil.

The bogs of the Black Mountains were well-known haunts of Will-o'-the-wisps, and, like the ridges around Coity Mountain in Blaenavon, have their own 'hag' as well as demonic crows. Sometimes, the crows of the mountain were known to put out travellers' lights, causing them

The old witch stood in the rector's churchyard surrounded by a group of figures. Moonlight shone straight through the bodies of the people, and he saw that she was conversing with the dead.

to lose their way. They were therefore assumed to be in league with the Devil.

It would seem that the witch, the Will-o'-the-wisps, the hag and the crows were somehow related, as their main purpose was to confuse, frustrate and endanger the lives of travellers.

Wirt Sikes (quoting the earlier folklorist Edmund Jones) reports that Robert Williams, of Langattock, Crickhowel, 'a substantial man and of undoubted veracity', told this tale. As he was travelling one night over part of the Black Mountain, he saw the Old Woman, and at the same time found he had lost his way. Not knowing her to be a spectre he hallooed to her to stay for him, but receiving no answer thought she was deaf. He then hastened his steps, thinking to overtake her, but the faster he ran the further he found himself behind her, at which he wondered very much, not knowing the reason of it. He presently found himself stumbling in a marsh, at which discovery his vexation increased, and then he heard the Old Woman laughing at him with a weird, uncanny, crackling old laugh. This set him to thinking she might be a gwyll;

and when he happened to draw out his knife for some purpose, and the Old Woman vanished, then he was sure of it, for Welsh ghosts and fairies are afraid of a knife.

If you undertake the suggested walk through Wiral Wood, remember this: you will be surrounded on all sides, above and below, by all manner of wild and dangerous 'things'.

Walk 21 – Wiral Wood

WALK INFORMATION:
START/PARKING: Llanthony Priory car park GR SO288278
RECOMMENDED MAP: OS Explorer OL13 or Landranger 161
DISTANCE (APPROX): 2km / 1.3 miles
TIME (APPROX): 1 hour
WALK TYPE: Circular
DIFFICULTY RATING: Easy
NOTES: Combine with a trip to nearby Hay Bluff (see *Lonely Moors and Sinister Hills*).

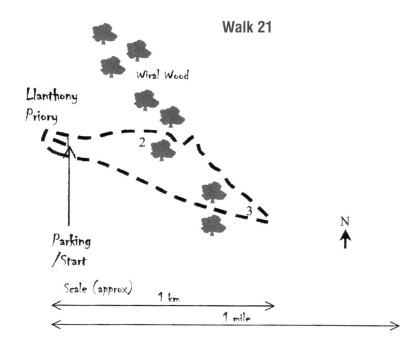

Walk 21

Wiral Wood

Llanthony Priory

Parking /Start

Scale (approx)

1 km

1 mile

N

1. Exit the car park and look out for a sign saying 'Hill Walks'. Go through a gate and turn right as directed by a fingerpost indicating 'Circular Walk Hateral Hill'. Turn right after a short distance to walk in the direction of a fingerpost indicting 'Offa's Dyke South'. Follow the priory wall to a gate leading into a field. Walk up through the field, go through the gate and enter Wiral Wood.

2. Follow a well-defined path up through the wood, ignoring a path leading off to the right. At a small stream bear right, ignoring a track leading off to the left, to reach a wooden gate. Follow the field boundary for a short distance to a stile leading into the field on the right. Cross the field in the direction indicated by the fingerpost, crossing a stream along the way until you arrive at a ruined cottage.

3. Double back on yourself slightly to enter the small woodland below via a stile. Walk through the wood in the direction indicted by the waymarker, taking care to avoid the electric fence further down in the wood to your left. Cross a stile next to a water tank and bear right in the direction indicted by the waymarker. Pass through a gate in the direction of the now visible priory ruins, crossing two small streams along the way. Eventually you will reach a farmyard. Go through the gate to follow the Public Right of Way through the farmyard, turning right at the road to return to the priory car park.

The Wood of the Pagan Cult

There stood a grove
Which from the earliest time no hand of man
Had dared to violate; hidden from the sun
Its chill recesses; matted boughs entwined
Prisoned the air within.
No sylvan nymphs
Here found a home, nor Pan, but savage rites
And barbarous worship, altars horrible
On massive stones upreared; sacred with blood
Of men was every tree.
(From *Pharsalia* by Marcus Annaeus Lucanus (Lucan))

You decide to take a walk. At first, it seems to be a fairly typical woodland. Then you arrive at a cliff face. As you get closer, strange carvings become apparent. Curious, you decide to take a closer look. Many faces, carved from the rock, stare back at you. They seem to be clustered around an odd-looking stone above a large slab. An altar? Suddenly, you remember the stories – Celtic head cults, sacrifices and sacred groves. As the darkness descends, the woods feel very different. You begin to feel nervous. This is a strange place.

Welcome to Tarren Deusant, a little-known natural rock feature in a woodland near Llantrisant, South Wales. Tarren Deusant translates as 'rock of the two saints'. The Royal Commission on the Ancient and Historic Monuments of Wales describes the site as 'rock carvings; possible holy well; Celtic pagan shrine'. If so, this would make some of the carvings Iron Age (i.e. pre-Roman).

The chilling figures and faces are carved into the rock in a south-facing cliff. Within the cliff is the so-called 'Druid's Altar', which consists of a lighter-coloured 'teardrop' or 'phallus' stone

that stands proud of the surrounding darker rock. Beneath this lies a flat area of rock reminiscent of an altar. Rock carvings surround the teardrop stone and a spring can be found near its base. It would seem that people are still using this site as a sacred grove of some kind, given the amount of candle wax and coin offerings around the altar.

In *Glamorgan Ghosts*, Viv Small tells an interesting story that adds a supernatural dimension to the wood. The story concerns a Llantrisant man who attended a wedding at Penycoedcae. After drinking all day, he made for home, refusing an offer from friends to stay the night. His friends had had some concerns about this, and warned him to stay on the road (which sounds like a familiar warning!).

Whilst walking along the road from Penycoedcae to Llantrisant he heard a voice in the darkness telling him to 'come here'. This happened a number of times, until curiosity got the better of him and he was coaxed from the road into a dark field. He stumbled through a black maze of twigs and branches, encouraged by the voice calling 'a little further'. Battered, bruised

One of many chilling faces carved into the rock at Tarren Deusant, a possible Celtic pagan shrine

The woods around Tarren Deusant lie in a steep-sided stream valley, and can be extremely unnerving, even in the daytime

and feeling the effects of the alcohol, the man decided to take a rest. Sleep took hold of him. Suddenly, he woke with the memory of the strange events of the evening before.

To his horror, he found he had fallen asleep on the edge of the cliff directly above the Druid's Altar. The voice in the darkness had tried to lure him to his death at the ancient site of sacrifice and worship.

Does Tarren Deusant still hunger for victims? Let's hope not.

Walk 22 – Tarren Deusant

START: Queen's Head pub, Penycoedcae GR ST 060878
PARKING: Roadside parking near pub
MAP: OS Explorer 166 or Landranger 170
DISTANCE (APPROX): 2.8km / 1.75 miles
TIME (APPROX): 1 hour
WALK TYPE: Linear
DIFFICULTY RATING: Easy
NOTES: Part of the route follows a diversion not shown on maps in 2007.

1. With your back to the car park of the Queen's Head pub, walk right down the lane. Just after Bron Y Garn barn look out for a stone stile in a stone wall on your left. Walk across the field and cross two more stiles to reach a large open field. Head for the top right-hand corner to a field gate next to the wood and a small stream. At the time of writing there was no stile so I had to climb over the locked gate. The farmer told me he would be looking to install a stile in the near future. Follow a track down to a small bridge and cross the stile.

2. Turn left, passing a gate on the left. After a few metres ascend uphill and right as directed by a waymarker. Follow the yellow waymarkers through the wood – the path roughly follows the stream on your left. You will soon find yourself walking downhill toward the cliff face. The rock carvings can be found toward the left-hand side. From here, retrace your steps upstream to return to the start point (the route is well waymarked in both directions).

The 'Druid's Altar'. There are at least eight faces carved into the rock, surrounding a strange tear-shaped stone.

A Midsummer Night's Nightmare

The Clydach Gorge can be found near Abergavenny, South Wales. This dramatic landform is three and a half miles in length and a half a mile wide, the deep river gorge dropping some 1,100 feet (330m) at its deepest point in the west. The gorge is famed for its natural beauty, dramatic waterfalls and caves. Cwm Clydach National Nature Reserve is the largest and most representative ancient beech woodland in south-east Wales.

Close to the river the air is humid, providing ideal conditions for the formation of mosses which contribute to the otherworldly feel of the place. The gorge is surely one of the most haunted places in Wales, being the abode of 'Pwccas' or goblins as well as a host of spectral entities.

Walk 22

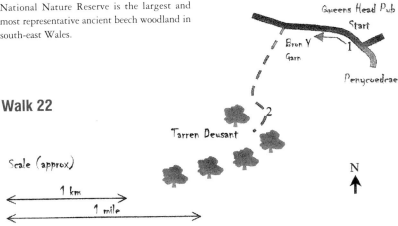

One story suggests a man was lured to Tarren Deusant by supernatural forces

Before the establishment of Clydach Ironworks, this was one of the most secluded spots in Wales and a well-known haunt of dangerous supernatural beings. It was said that the presence of the Pwccas was somewhat reduced with the coming of industry, but they didn't entirely desert their ancient habitat.

A man living near the gorge (part of which was once known as Cwm Pwcca or Pwcca's Valley) had a close encounter with one of these 'malicious goblins', and nearly lost his life. He was returning home via a nearby mountain late one night when he saw a strange light in the distance, 'which seemed to proceed from a candle in a lantern'.

Looking more closely, he saw that it was being carried by a figure that seemed to be taking the same route he intended to take. He therefore decided to catch the fellow up so that he could benefit from the safety of his lantern, along what was a very steep and rocky path down into the valley.

Although the man with the lantern seemed to be very short, he was moving at a remarkable pace. Despite this, the miner was determined to catch up with him. The route soon took a turn for the worse, and he became worried because

he wasn't familiar with the track.

Eventually the miner caught up with the little man with the lantern, but to his horror found himself at the edge of one of the tremendous precipices of Cwm Pwcca. One more step and death would be assured in the roaring torrents of the river below. As he stopped short of the precipice, the little lantern man performed the superhuman feat of springing across the gorge to the other side whilst holding the light above his head. He turned around to face the miner, roared with malicious laughter and disappeared up the hill opposite.

It seems Shakespeare heard about Cwm Pwcca's fame as the abode of supernatural beings. The story goes that he came here for inspiration and to write his play, *A Midsummer Night's Dream*. Shakespeare is said to have spent a great deal of time in the area, and based his famous character, Puck, on the Pwccas of the gorge. Locals would enthusiastically point out where Shakespeare was supposed to have stayed, and a cave in the ravine east of Lower Fedw Ddu is still known as 'Shakespeare's Cave'. Likewise, visitors were once shown a cave where a belated miner was 'kept dancing for ten years' by the fairies of the gorge (this may be the same cave).

Cwm Clydach was once known as 'Cwm Pwcca', and is the abode of 'Pwccas' or goblins, as well as a host of spectral entities. It is thought that Shakespeare visited the gorge for inspiration whilst writing A Midsummer Night's Dream.

The Pwccas weren't entirely confined to the gorge. Nearby, a Pwcca was kept in the employ of a local farmer. This particular Pwcca's physical form was said to have been that of a giant human nose!

In addition to Pwccas, numerous spirits haunt the gorge. The Saleyard Bridge is haunted by a headless horseman and a disappearing walker, and nearby Cwm Siôn Mathew is haunted by a Gwyllgi or 'Hound of Hell'.

Walk 23 – Clydach Gorge

START/PARKING: Gilwern Wharf Car Park GR SO242147
MAP: 1:25,000 OS Explorer OL13 or Landranger 161
DISTANCE: 5km / 3 miles
TIME: 1.5 to 2 hours
WALK TYPE: Circular
DIFFICULTY RATING: Moderate
NOTES: Cwm Pwcca can be viewed from Devil's Bridge. The bridge is easily accessible from the Drum and Monkey pub, Blackrock, Clydach GR

SO216125. Go through a gate just after the pub on the right-hand side, go through a subway and turn right to cross a stile. Follow the path downhill to reach Devil's Bridge.

1. Facing the canal, turn right to follow the towpath. Go through a kissing gate and pass under a stone bridge. Continue to the next bridge, pass under it and look for a stone stile on the right. Cross the stile, turn right and cross the bridge in the direction of Llanelly Church. Follow the path to the right then left as it ascends the hill. Continue up the steep hill until you reach a metalled road near the church.

2. Turn left along the road and then right to walk around the churchyard wall in a clockwise direction. Turn left at a 'Church Road' sign. Continue to Neuadd Farm and look out for a gate and two fingerposts on your right, immediately after the farm (easy to miss). Go through the gate and turn left as indicated by one of the fingerposts. You will need to walk around a fence to follow the line of the Public Footpath. Go through a gate,

Walk 23

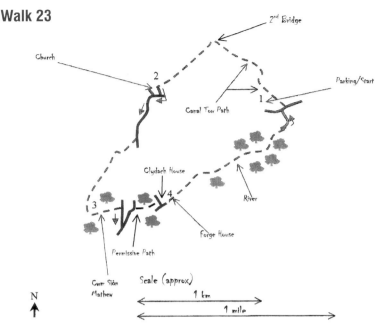

2nd Bridge

Church

Parking/Start

2

1

Canal Tow Path

Clydach House

4

River

3

Forge House

Permissive Path

Cwm Siôn Mathew

Scale (approx)

1 km

1 mile

N

cross a field and cross a stile. Continue straight on with the fence to your left and cross two more stiles and a stream. The stream is difficult to negotiate because of the eroded banks (you will need to scramble up the opposite bank). Continue with the fence line to your left, passing a stile on your left to reach a gate and stile next to some stone walls. Cross the stile and continue straight on towards some trees. Look out for a stile on the left just before you reach the Gwyllgi-haunted Cwm Siôn Mathew.

3. Cross the stile and go through a gap in a stone wall. Continue down through the field keeping the stream to the right (watch out for steep drops near the bottom). Cross a stile onto the road and turn right. At a junction, turn left and follow the road for a short distance around some bends to reach a wooded area on the right. Look out for a stile on the right (a permissive path). Cross the stile and walk down through the wood to reach Clydach House, where you need to turn right down the road for a very short distance and then left at a junction. Continue down the road, passing the haunted Saleyard Bridge on your right, to reach Forge House.

4. Continue straight along a narrow path between hedges to reach a bridge and waterfall on the right just after a Welsh Water hut on the left. Take a look at the waterfalls (note the strange atmosphere), double back and continue along your original route to reach a fingerpost on the right at the end of some railings. Follow this path through woodland with the river to your right. Eventually you will reach a road. Turn left then right at a junction near a cottage. Cross the road at the next junction, turn right over the canal bridge, then left to return to the start point.

The Haunted Grove

Tinkinswood and St. Lythans are some of the most remarkable and mysterious Stone Age burial chambers (cromlechs) in Wales. They lie adjacent to some wonderful mature wooded groves near St Nicholas in the Vale of Glamorgan.

Tinkinswood dates to around 3500 BC and was in use until 2000 BC. Hundreds of bones were found interred within the chamber, representing the remains of up to 40 people.

Late one evening, a 'malicious goblin' of the gorge tried to lure a miner to his death

The capstone is thought to be the biggest of its type in Europe and would have needed huge resources to lift into place. A nearby stone row hints that this was once a larger ritual and funerary complex.

Although Tinkinswood predates the time of the Celts, the spirits of long-dead Druids haunt the site. In *Folk-Lore and Folk-Stories of Wales,* Marie Trevelyan describes how the spirits punish drunkards and sinners: 'A man fond of drink slept there one night, and his experiences were terrible. He declared the Druids beat him first, and then whirled him up to the sky, from which he looked down and saw the moon and stars thousands of miles below him. The Druids held him suspended by his hair in the mid-heaven,

Many people have reported strange experiences when in proximity to Tinkinswood burial chamber

until the first peep of day, and then let him drop down to the Dyffryn woods, where he was found in a great oak by farm-labourers.'

Dancing on the Sabbath near the stones can also have dire consequences. The group of stones to the south of the site are said to have been women turned to stone for their indiscretions.

The power of the site shouldn't be underestimated. Spending the night in the tomb on one of the three 'spirit nights' (May Day's Eve, Midsummer Eve and Midwinter Eve) could result in death and madness. Indeed, many people claim to have experienced strange dreams and visions whilst sleeping in proximity to Tinkinswood.

In *British Goblins*, Wirt Sikes suggests that a local name for Tinkinswood – Castle Correg – is likely to have derived from the Breton Korreds and Korregs, cromlech fairies who dance at night and were believed to have been the builders of the great monuments.

Nearby St Lythans is a smaller but very similar burial chamber that has never been excavated. In common with a number of such monuments, it was once known as Gwal y Filiast (the Greyhound-Bitch Kennel).

The capstone is said to spin around three times on Midsummer's Eve and the stones go down to the river to drink. If you whisper a wish to the stones on a Halloween night they will be granted.

The field in which the St Lythans burial chamber stands is said to be 'unprofitable' and 'cursed'. A horse that gallops around in the moonlight haunts the field. If you attempt to ride it, the story insists you'll be sorry...

Walk 24 – Tinkinswood and St Lythans

START/PARKING: GR ST097732 Follow signs to Tinkinswood from St Nicholas
RECOMMENDED MAP: OS Explorer 151 or Landranger 170
DISTANCE (APPROX): 4km / 2.5 miles
TIME (APPROX): 1 to 1.5 hours
WALK TYPE: Circular
DIFFICULTY RATING: Easy
NOTES: Take care walking along narrow country lanes.
1. The route to Tinkinswood is well waymarked.

From the lay-by go through a kissing gate and turn left to follow the field boundary in the direction indicted. Tinkinswood burial chamber can be accessed via a kissing gate near the monument. After visiting the monument, cross a stile and then another near some standing stones. Walk across a field as indicted by a waymarker, passing a wooden electricity pylon to cross another stile near some oak trees. Walk diagonally right across the field and cross a stile next to a paddock. Cross a field in the direction indicated by a waymarker. Go through a field gate to follow a rough track to a gate and stile near some sheds. Cross the stile and continue in the direction of the pylons to reach a stream and a stile next to a stone wall leading onto the road. Turn left along the road then left again.

2. Follow the road, passing Dyffryn Woods on your left, eventually passing a junction on your left leading back to the start point (don't turn up the road quite yet). Continue uphill as indicted by a road sign saying 'St Lythans Burial Chamber'. You will soon see a sign directing you right off the road to St Lythans. Go through the kissing gate via the haunted field to reach the monument.

3. Retrace your steps to the road and turn left to return to the junction. Turn right and follow the road back to the start point, passing the main entrance to Dyffryn Gardens on the way.

Devil Dog Lane

If you want to experience the terror of an encounter with a Gwyllgi (Hell Hound), this is the place. The tiny village of Llysworney lies two miles west of Cowbridge in the Vale of Glamorgan.

A terrifying half-human, half-dog with glowing eyes haunts a lane between the farm of Crossways and a place called Mousiad (no longer on the map, unless the word is a derivative of Moorshead). A farmer by the name of Jenkin, from Wilton Farm, was returning home through the lane on his mare one evening. He was feeling rather flustered, having come from a day at the local market. Suddenly, the mare reared up, threw the startled Jenkin off, and then galloped

Walk 24

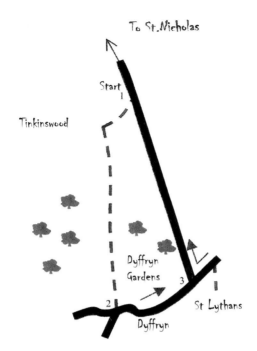

To St.Nicholas

Start
1

Tinkinswood

Dyffryn
Gardens
3

2

St Lythans

Dyffryn

Scale (approx)

1 km

1 mile

N

home without him.

Seeing the mare return, the residents of the farm set off to see what had happened to the old farmer. They eventually found him on his back in the mud, swearing that a Gwyllgi had frightened his horse.

A farm servant called Anthony (one of the searchers in the first story) saw the Gwyllgi for himself. One Sunday night he was on his way home when he saw two moon-like eyes approaching. When it got closer he saw that the head and upper body were of human form, whilst the body and legs were of a large, bright-spotted dog.

It may be of relevance that the farm adjacent to the wooded lane in question (Breach Farm)

is full of Bronze Age archaeology in the form of a barrow cemetery. Throughout Britain, the Hounds of Hell or Black Dogs are reckoned to be the appointed guardians of Bronze Age sites.

In *Folk Lore and Folk Stories from Wales*, Marie Trevelyan adds: 'Near Wilton Crossways, in the Vale of Glamorgan, one of these spirit-hounds was frequently to be seen even so late as a "few years ago". This creature is described as having features and upper part of the body of semihuman form. The other part and lower limbs were those of a "light-spotted dog". The eyes were large and "like moons", and sometimes "smoke came out of its mouth". This animal made unearthly howlings, and "glared fiercely", render-

89

A drunkard attempted to spend the night in Tinkinswood burial chamber. As punishment the spirits of long-dead Druids beat him and held him suspended by his hair in the mid-heaven, until the first peep of day, and then let him drop down to the Dyffryn woods, where he was found in a great oak by farm labourers.

ing people senseless with his glances.'

Trevelyan (real name Emma Mary Thomas) grew up in the Vale of Glamorgan and may have heard about local Hell Hounds at first hand. She says that '"as late as forty years ago", people would speak "with bated breath" about a pack of phantom hounds that would tear along the road between Marlborough Grange and Nash Manor. If you were unfortunate enough to meet the hounds your clothes would be torn to pieces and you would be "almost left for dead".'

As if the aforementioned terrors weren't bad enough, 'another roadway in the same locality is haunted by a terrible coal-black dog, with eyes

St Lythans burial chamber lies within a cursed and haunted field

A terrifying half-human, half-dog Gwyllgi with glowing eyes haunts this green lane near Breach Farm Bronze Age barrow cemetery

like balls of fire. This creature is said to follow people like a footpad, and to snarl and howl if any person halts or looks backward'. Don't look behind you!

Walk 25 – Llysworney

START: Carne Arms, Llysworney GR SS963740
PARKING: Roadside parking near pub
MAP: 1:25,000 OS Explorer 151 or Landranger 170
DISTANCE (APPROX): 5km / 3 miles
TIME (APPROX): 1.5 hours
WALK TYPE: Part circular
DIFFICULTY RATING: Easy
NOTES: Take care when crossing roads and walking along country lanes.

1. From the Carne Arms (facing the road), turn right along the pavement on the right hand side of the road. Turn right up a country lane where the path narrows at Pen y lan cottage (take great care here). Follow the road to a crossroads near a bend in the road (just after a wooden electricity pylon), then turn right onto the Gwyllgi-haunted green lane. Follow the lane to a road and turn left to reach a main road. Cross the road with care and go through a gap in the hedge at the edge of a field. Cross the field to reach a stone stile in the left-hand corner (near a cowshed).

2. Cross the stile and walk parallel to the road to reach a stile next to a gate. Cross the stile and turn left to cross a stile leading onto the road. Turn right and continue along the road, passing a track to New Breach Farm on the left (watch out for cars as the road is narrow in places). Pass Moorshead Farm and turn right at the junction where a sign indicates 'Cowbridge Bont faen 3 ¾. Just after Wilton Farm (Wilton House), turn right up a bank with a rail and some wooden steps.

3. Cross a double stile and walk across a field in the direction of the waymarker, passing a ruined building on the right to reach another double stile. Cross this and walk across the field, keeping close to the corner of the wooded copse on your left. You should be able to see Nash Manor to your left. Look out for a double stile in the hedge ahead. Cross the stile and turn right to follow the field boundary towards the cowsheds you passed earlier. Turn left near the road to return to the stone stile you crossed earlier. Cross the field and re-cross the main

A pack of phantom hounds is known to tear along the road between Marlborough Grange and Nash Manor (centre)

road via the gap in the hedge, then walk back down Penrheol Terrace. Shortly after, turn right for another pass through the haunted lane, then turn left at the crossroads. At the end of the lane, turn left along the narrow path back into the village (take great care as your back will be to oncoming traffic).

Further Exploration

More Haunted Woods, UFOs and Hell Hounds

There are many more haunted woods and wooded lanes to be discovered. Here are a few more suggestions...

The Old Ghost Road

Lôn y Bwbach near Llandeddyfnan, Anglesey, means 'Lane of the Goblin' and was named due to the weird effect the haunted lane could have on animals . Horses would become highly distressed, and fall down in a fit, and it was presumed this was a result of a malevolent presence in the lane.

In *Haunted Wales*, Richard Holland explains that a number of theories were put forward to explain the presence. A leading explanation for the haunting concerned the lord of Plas Llanddyfnan during the Civil War – a certain Mr Griffiths. He was a prominent loyalist and was killed by Parliamentarian forces whilst trying to make his escape along the lane. He was said to have suffered a cruel death, and before long the lane gained its name and sinister reputation.

The lane is still clearly marked on OS maps as Lôn y Bwbach (track). The lines of old walls and hedges still define the route and trees crowd the lane, forming a spooky tunnel effect. It would take some courage to make the walk alone, in darkness.

The lane is easily accessed from the 'Stone Science' museum on the B5109, just outside Pentraeth. You can walk through much of the lane, but it is best to turn back when you reach a house as the Public Right of Way runs along the driveway.

I would suggest combining a visit to Lôn y Bwbach with a visit to Llyn Cerrig Bach. This lake is possibly the most important pre-Roman Iron Age (Celtic) ritual site in Britain. More than 150 bronze and iron objects were found here – thrown in as votive offerings. It is thought that human and animal sacrifice may also have taken place here. Roman soldiers and robed figures haunt the lakeshore.

Walk 25

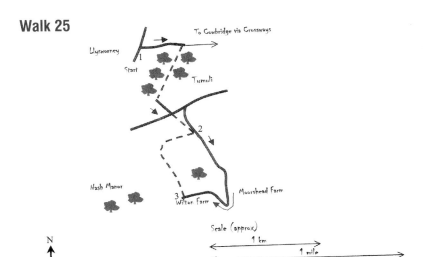

Little Wood, Big Frights

Coed Bach ('little wood') lies near the road between Llanerfyl and Llangadfan. It is haunted by 'a shadowy figure of a dignified lady', 'agonising shrieks' and spectral lights that look like lighted windows.

Hafren Forest

Hafren Forest can be found on the lower slopes of the Pumlumon massif. During the 1987 Welsh 'flap', the forest was the setting for some *X-Files*-type UFO weirdness. Strange black 'flying triangles' were reported on a regular basis, and unexplained 'strobe lights' were seen in and around the forest. This led to concern about activities taking place within a 'secret' British Aerospace facility, located deep within Hafren.

Stories circulated about the curious UFO buffs being escorted away from the facility by sinister security personnel. At the time, British Aerospace refused to tell locals what was going on, but they did admit that a quarry site deep within the forest had been chosen due to its distance from domestic and industrial electromagnetic 'smog'. The facility is now a Centre for Explosion Studies in connection with Aberystwyth University's Combustion Physics Group.

The Ghost Lights of St Julian's Wood

St Julian's Wood can be found along the road between the ancient Roman fortress of Caerleon and the city of Newport in south-east Wales. Mysterious lights have been seen in these woods for many years, up until fairly recently. This area is full of history, now largely forgotten. Once, St Julian's formed a part of a great forest stretching many miles towards the Forest of Dean.

Nearby lie the remains of a small Iron Age hill fort (St Julian's Wood Hill Fort), which no doubt fell into disuse with the coming of the Romans. Above the wood an ancient ridgeway ran in the direction of Wentwood Forest.

St Julian's Wood was traditionally where Christians from the nearby legionary fortress of Caerleon were brought to be killed under the religious persecutions of Emperor Diocletian. Although initially tolerant of Christianity, in AD 303 he issued an edict in which he prohibited it. This brought about numerous executions between 303 and 311 involving the confiscation of property and the destruction of churches.

The real reason for the persecution was not because of their Christian faith itself, but because the Christians refused to offer sacrifices to the Roman deities and to the Emperor as a god. In the mind of the Emperor this risked jeopardising the prosperity and divine protection of the Empire. Usually they got to choose between making an offering to Roman pagan deities or being executed.

The old mansion of St Julian's (destroyed by modern housing developments) was the one-time residence of the 'father' of Deism, Lord Herbert of Cherbury. The mansion was said to have been built near the site of a chapel dedicated to the martyr, Julius.

In his *De Excidio Britanniae*, (Concerning the Ruin of Britain) the sixth-century monk Gildas says, 'God in the time of persecution lest Britain should be completely enveloped in the thick darkness of black night, kindled for us bright lamps of holy martyrs. The graves where their bodies lie, and the places of their suffering, had they not, very many of them, been taken from us the citizens on account of our numerous crimes, through the disastrous division caused by the barbarians, would at the present time inspire the minds of those who gazed at them with a far from feeble glow of divine love. I speak of Saint Alban of Verulam, Aaron and Julius, citizens of Caerleon, and the rest of both sexes in different places, who stood firm with lofty nobleness of mind in Christ's battle.'

St Julian's Wood is haunted by many flickering torch lights. These are said to be the torches of the relatives of slaughtered Christians searching for their loved ones amongst the woods. They were seen in the 1940s, but were interpreted as King Arthur and his knights, coming to Britain's rescue at the outbreak of World War II. I have also come across a number of vague reports regarding odd balls of light or orbs in and around these woods in recent times.

Old Wentwood

'And through the Usk they came to the forest.' So begins King Arthur's magical journey from Caerleon in the tale of 'Geraint, son of Erbin' from the *Mabinogion*. Wentwood is a fascinating place. This is the largest ancient woodland in Wales, a vestige of a vast wood that once divided the ancient kingdom of Gwent into Gwent Uwchcoed and Iscoed (Gwent above the wood and Gwent under the wood). The area is rich in Bronze Age archaeology, and an astonishing megalithic alignment can be found on Grey Hill.

A one-time hunting forest, Wentwood was known for its 'six castles' – at least one of which is now an archetypal 'forgotten ruin'. I once read an old poem referring to 'the haunted paths of Wentwood', and I'm confident there are many chilling tales to be told about the forest. I have personally heard about the sound of phantom horsemen, disappearing aeroplanes and numerous UFO reports. Wentwood is said to be a 'breeding ground' for Alien Big Cats in the area. The natural history, history and folklore of the forest would make a worthy book in itself.

The Hell Hound Wood

In *Folklore of Gwent*, T A Davies tells a strange tail concerning Hygga Wood (Hygga Dingle), near Llanishen, Monmouthshire. An old countryman told Davies that his parents could summon the Hounds of Hell using a conjurer's book or grimoire. The old countryman went on to relate: 'At Hygga Wood, you would hear the Hell Hounds making their music.' It seems the area around Llanishen and Trellech were well-known haunts of the hounds.

This well-wooded landscape is still the haunt of strange creatures. Wild boar have been spotted in the area and a red deer was recently seen in nearby woods (the animal obligingly left unmistakable tracks). Recently, I have heard (on good authority) that lynx tracks have been found in the area. Indeed, Trellech was the scene of one of Britain's most famous Alien Big Cat encounters.

In August 2000 an eleven-year-old boy needed treatment after being 'mauled' by a large black cat. Earlier in the book it was noted that ABCs and Hell Hounds are eerily similar in terms of their nature and habitats. Can the Hell Hounds still be heard? There is only one way to find out…

Bibliography

Barber, Chris, *Mysterious Wales*, Blorenge Books, 1999

Berwyn Mountain UFO incident: http://en.wikipedia.org/w/index.php?title=Berwyn_Mountain_UFO_incident&oldid=120491334 (accessed 20 April 2007)

Big Cats: www.bbc.co.uk/wales/southeast/sites/weird/pages/bigcats.shtml (accessed 20 March 2007)

Blaenau Gwent County Borough Council, *Folklore of Blaenau Gwent*, 1991

Bord, Janet & Colin, *Modern Mysteries of Britain*, Diamond Books, 1987

Bord, Janet, *Fairies: Real Encounters with Little People* Michael O'Mara Books, 1997

Carreg y Bwci: www.tellmeabout.co.uk/stuff/Paranormal/Secrets-in-the-stones.asp (accessed 20 Mar 2007)

Clark, J H, *History of Monmouthshire*, Usk, 1869

Cooper, Susan, *The Grey King*, Puffin Books, 1977

Croker, Thomas Crofton, *Fairy Legends and Traditions of the South of Ireland*, Vol 2 (1828)

Dancing mountain ghost: www.bbc.co.uk/wales/northeast/guides/weird/ghosts/pages/moel_famau.shtml (accessed 20 March 2007)

Davies, T A, 'Folklore of Gwent: Monmouthshire Legends and Traditions,' *Folklore*, 49 (1937)

Devereux, Paul, *Earth Lights Revelation*, Blandford Press, 1989

Devereux, Paul, *Earth Lights*, Turnstone Press, 1982

Devereux, Paul, *Places of Power*, Blandford Press, 1990

Devereux, Paul, *Symbolic Landscapes: The Dreamtime Earth and Aveburys's Open Secrets*, Gothic Image Publications, 1992

Ellison, A J, 'A romantic fiction', *The Unexplained*, Orbis Publishing, 1992

Evans, Hilary, 'The Ripperston Farm riddle', *The Unexplained,* Orbis Publishing, 1992

Evans, Hilary, 'The story of the "Welsh triangle",' *The Unexplained*, Orbis Publishing, 1992

Evans, Hilary, 'The truth about the Welsh triangle', *The Unexplained*, Orbis Publishing, 1992

Fflint Central – Scrapbook: The Red House: www.fflintcentral.co.uk/RedHouse.htm (accessed 20 April 2007)

Fisher, Catherine, *The Candle Man*, Bodley Head Children's Books, 1994

Flying Saucery: www.uk-ufo.org/condign/berwart2.htm (accessed 20 March 2007)

Frere, Mary, *Old Deccan Days*, London, 1868

Griffiths, Brian S, *Secret and Sacred Beacons*, Gwasg Carreg Gwalch, 2002

Hafren Forest: http://en.wikipedia.org/w/index.php?title=Hafren_Forest&oldid=111890610 (accessed 20 April 2007)

Harte, Jeremy, 'Alternative Approaches to Folklore 1969–1996' and 'Research in Geomancy 1990–1994': www.hoap.co.uk/download.htm (accessed 20 March 2007)

Historic Landscape Characterisation: The Tanat Valley: www.cpat.org.uk/projects/longer/histland/tanat/tanat.htm (accessed 20 March 2007)

Historical Trails Around the Great Orme, Conwy County Borough Council

Holland, Richard, *Haunted Wales*, Landmark Publishing, 2005

Holland, Richard, *Wales of the Unexpected*, Gwasg Carreg Gwalch, 2005

Hotbed of sightings: www.bbc.co.uk/wales/northeast/guides/weird/ufos/pages/gt_orme.shtml (accessed 20 March 2007)

Innes, Simon, 'Beware of the Dog', *The Unexplained*, Orbis Publishing, 1992

Innes, Simon, 'Tracking down black dogs', *The Unexplained*, Orbis Publishing, 1992

Jeffrey, P H, *Ghosts and Legends of Wales*, Old Orchard Press, 1990

Jones, Edmund, *A Relation of Apparitions of Spirits in the County of Monmouth and the Principality of Wales* 1767 (repr. Trefeca, 1780; 2nd repr. Newport, 1813)

Jones, T Gwyn, *Welsh Folk Lore and Custom*, Methuen, 1930

Main, Laurence, *The Spirit Paths of Wales*, Cicerone Press, 2000

Marsdon, Simon, *The Haunted Realm*, Little, Brown & Company, 1998

Muir, Hazel, 'Blackholes in your backyard', *New Scientist* 2583 (3 January 2007)

Mystery Light Seen Across Wales: http://news.bbc.co.uk/1/hi/wales/north_west/6294099.stm (accessed 20 March 2007)

Owen, Elias, *Welsh Folk-Lore*, Woodall, Minshall & Co, 1896

Palmer, Roy, *The Folklore of (Old) Monmouthshire*, Logaston Press, 1998

Paranormal Database: www.paranormaldatabase.com (accessed 20 March 2007)

Playfair, Lyon, 'In search of apparitions', *The Unexplained*, Orbis Publishing, 1992

Pugh, Jane, *Welsh Ghosts and Phantoms*, Emerelda, 1993

Randles, Jenny, *Time Storms*, Piatkus, 2001

Randles, Jenny, *UFO Reality*, Robert Hale, 1983

Randles, Jenny, *UFOs and How to See Them*, Anaya Publishers, 1992

Redfern, Nick, *A Covert Agenda*, Simon & Schuster, 1997

Redfern, Nick, *Six Weeks in Pursuit of Werewolves, Lake Monsters, Giant Cats, Ghostly Devil Dogs and Ape Men*, Paraview Pocket Books, 2004

Rhys, John, *Celtic Folklore*, Clarendon Press, 1901

Roderick, Alan, *Unknown Gwent*, Village, 1986

Sikes, Wirt, *British Goblins*, Sampson Low, 1880

Slemen, Tom, *Haunted Liverpool 3*, The Bluecoat Press, 1998

Small, Vivian, *Glamorgan Ghosts: Ghost Stories from Seashore to Mountain Top: and Some from Just Down the Road*, The Small Book Company, 2004

Smyth, Frank, 'Ghosts without souls?', *The Unexplained*, Orbis Publishing, 1992

Smyth, Frank, 'Understanding ghosts', *The Unexplained*, Orbis Publishing, 1992

Soldier of doom: www.bbc.co.uk/wales/northeast/guides/weird/ghosts/pages/roman.shtml (accessed 20 March 2007)

Styles, Showell, *The Mountains of North Wales*, Gollancz, 1971

Tarren deussant: www.coflein.gov.uk/pls/portal/coflein.w_details?inumlink=6057825 (accessed 20 March 2007)

Thomas, W J, *The Welsh Fairy Book*, Unwin, 1907

Titcombe, Colin, *Wildlife in Gwent Post Millennium*, self-published 2006

Tongues of flames: www.bbc.co.uk/wales/northeast/guides/weird/ufos/pages/moelfre.shtml (accessed 20 March 2007)

Trevelyan, Marie, *Folk-Lore and Folk-Stories of Wales*, Elliot Stock, 1909

Uney, Graham, *The High Summits of Wales*, Logaston Press, 1999

Watkins, Alfred: *The Old Straight Track*, Methuen, 1925

Weird Wales: www.bbc.co.uk/wales/weird/ (accessed 20 April 2007)

Werewolves: www.bbc.co.uk/wales/northeast/guides/weird/mythsandlegends/pages/werewolf.shtml (accessed 20 March 2007)